D0458392

Coming Back

Coming

Back

A PSYCHIATRIST EXPLORES PAST-LIFE JOURNEYS

Raymond A. Moody, Jr., M.D.
with Paul Perry

BANTAM BOOKS
NEW YORK · TORONTO · LONDON · SYDNEY · AUCKLAND

All rights reserved.
Copyright © 1990 *by Raymond A. Moody, Jr.*
No part of this book may be reproduced or transmitted
in any form or by any means, electronic or mechanical,
including photocopying, recording, or by any information
storage and retrieval system, without permission in
writing from the publisher.
For information address: Bantam Books.

Published simultaneously in the United States and Canada

Bantam Books are published by Bantam Books, a division of Bantam Doubleday Dell
Publishing Group, Inc. Its trademark, consisting of the words "Bantam Books" and the
portrayal of a rooster, is Registered in U.S. Patent and Trademark Office and in other
countries. Marca Registrada. Bantam Books, 666 Fifth Avenue, New York, New York
10103.

PRINTED IN THE UNITED STATES OF AMERICA

CONTENTS

Introduction

Have we lived before? Do we live again?

Many people, religious and nonreligious alike, believe that we do. Hindus think that we die and return in a sort of endless cycle of death and renewal. Some Orientals, for instance, believe that if you are laden with sin when you die, you will return again as a human in order to be given the chance to purify yourself. Hindus believe that you shall reap as you sow: a bad person in this life comes back as something unappealing, such as an insect, in the next.

Some people believe that they can return to those past lives almost at will. They believe that hypnosis can tap an area of the brain that stores all or part of the lives they have lived like a file cabinet stores old tax records.

This process of hypnotically getting at these past lives is called *past-life regression.*

I think it is safe to say that most people consider regression bogus. They link it with such beliefs as harmonic convergences (where the planets line up to form power zones on the earth), or the healing of diseases through the use of crystals.

There are significant differences between these things (which I too consider bogus) and past-life regression. The main difference is this: using the vehicle of past-life regression, *something happens.* Normal, psychologically healthy people actually see themselves in ancient cultures, living lives in long-ago eras. They find themselves wearing the dress of the period and often find themselves surrounded by conversation of the time.

Not everyone who regresses finds himself living the life of Christopher Columbus, Henry VIII, or some other famous historical figure. Most aren't royalty or members of the elite. For the most part, they are slaves or gladiators, soldiers or stable boys. In short, they are ordinary folk living lives as ordinary as the ones they lead now. Few are special people and even fewer experience lives of opulence and grandeur.

I know this is true because I have seen it in my own psychiatric practice.

From time to time, while working as a psychotherapist with psychologically healthy human beings, I have been surprised to hear patients describe puzzling episodes during which they seemed to be transported back through time and space to a realm where they experienced a sense of identity with an individual who lived in an earlier historical period.

Usually the experience takes the form of a sensory image. Most often it is visual. But sometimes the person being hypnotized describes only sounds and smells and can see nothing. They feel that these images relate to events that happened before they were born. Yet these images seem so real that the individuals are convinced they were actually "back in time."

For a long time I assumed that the handful of cases I had treated or heard of were aberrations, just brief vivid daydreams not worthy of serious investigation.

And that's where I would have left it, had it not been for the publication of Life After Life, my first book on near-death experiences. After the publication of that book, I received hundreds of letters from readers. Most of them described near-death experiences, vivid spiritual experiences of people who had almost died.

But among those letters were reports of other types of fascinating psychological and spiritual phenomena, including numerous accounts of past-life recollections similar to the ones I had heard described by patients in psychotherapy. Some of them, like the following, were amazing:

When I was regressed I found myself as a little girl of about twelve in the forest standing by a body of water. I looked down at my feet and noticed that they were dark. Next to me on a sort of cot was a woman I knew to be my grandmother. She was dying and I was feeling very alone.

I was able to regress further, back to about five years old. I had no sense of a father being present in the family, but I was there with my mother. All around us the men of the village were building these log houses. I spent my days with the women of the tribe, weaving baskets and gathering food.

I didn't know where this place was, but I knew that the white man was there because conversations told of being chased to this new place by white outsiders.

When my grandmother died I became a loner and lived by myself in the forest until my early twenties. Then I was able to go to my death scene and could see that I broke my leg and had no one to take care of me. I could see my leg become discolored and finally I realized that this was how I died.

This woman told me that her experiences were very vivid, just like recent memory. She said smells of her surroundings were even present.

Another woman found herself in a crowded marketplace with her father:

We had on rough robes and there were carts and horses all around. We stopped at a slave market where my father bought several slaves.

I was able to return to my home where I lived with my father. We had an elegant house with thick walls and beautiful furniture. I had the sense that we were very rich.

I went ahead in my life to the age of sixteen and found myself very upset at my father. He was trying to get me to marry an older man and I didn't want to do it. I was full of fury and fear.

I decided to go away to the New World. The woman who was my governess sneaked me some money and I bought passage on a boat that was crossing the ocean to America. But the boat sank. I could see all the people around me in panic and could see us all swimming desperately around looking for something to hang onto. Then I saw myself drowning.

As you can tell, these cases are similar in many ways. In the typical case, the person becomes flooded with images that he or she thinks pertain to his or her own life in an earlier time.

Although these images often occur in the context of a psychological conflict or life crisis, they sometimes seem to emerge for no reason.

Some of the letters I've received and the patients I've treated report these images after visiting a new geographic location. They say that the familiarity of the surroundings left them with nagging feelings that, as one letterwriter put it, "there are memories in those walls."

This spontaneous familiarity breeds a sense of nostalgia in many of these people. They often long for the surroundings seen in their regression. Did they live well in their earlier lives? Were they happy? Were they rich or poor? Were they well-respected pillars of the community? Or were they merely salt of the earth? Questions like these often come to mind when this window on the past is opened. For many, such an experience has heralded the beginning of a deep spiritual and psychological search, one which has ultimately resulted in a new sense of peace and self-understanding.

AN ODYSSEY FOR ALL

In recent years, past-life experiences have been widely discussed in the media. Shirley MacLaine had several of them which she recounts in vivid detail in *Out on a Limb*.

Her accounts of these "past-life" journeys—and the accountings of others—left most people thinking that they could only listen as others told of their remarkable hypnotic trips. To the rest of us, these doors of perception were closed.

So I thought too, until two years ago when I began to undertake my own personal journey into the baffling and exhila-rating realm of past-life experiences. Although I had spent much of my professional career studying the unusual experiences of others, nothing this extraordinary had ever happened to me.

And although I was trained in hypnosis, I had never used it for any purpose other than to help my patients learn how to relax, cope with pain, or stop smoking. Nor had I thought that I was a particularly good subject for hypnosis. For me, hypnosis was a way to deep relaxation, easy sleep, and nothing more.

But in April of 1986, the doors of perception were opened to me while I was visiting my friends John Audette and Diana Denholm in Florida. Diana is a clinical psychologist who has used hypnosis for years to help her clients lose weight, stop smoking, overcome phobias, and learn to relax.

She told me that every once in a while, a deeply hypnotized client would spontaneously regress to what they thought was a past life. The first time this happened was a puzzling experience for Diana. She thought she had made some kind of mistake, or that the patient had a multiple-personality disorder.

After it happened a few times, however, Diana was no longer frightened when people slipped far back into time. Instead she became intrigued by it and eventually learned how to induce a past-life regression.

Now, she told me, she used it as a therapeutic tool. She claimed that this "glimpse into the past" allowed patients to examine the problems they were having in the here and now.

I expressed skepticism to Diana. Like most in my profession, I didn't believe there was any validity in these claims of hypnotic time travel.

Without arguing she offered to hypnotize me. That afternoon she did. Under her patient guidance I went into a deep hypnotic trance and had an experience that was simply astounding. When asked about the experience now, I describe it as stirring, gripping, puzzling, yet ultimately very calming and reassuring.

EXPLORING A MYSTERY

What I experienced that day was the beginning of a fascinating two-year research project during which I have undergone numerous past-life regressions and have led dozens of individuals through the process of experiencing regressions themselves.

My investigation has led me to believe that almost anyone can experience these dramatic past-life journeys. It takes only patience and the willingness to believe that much remains unknown about the human mind, especially in the remarkable ways that it seems to communicate with itself. This is a dimension of the mind that has not been investigated to any great degree. But it is one that creates the personal myths in each of us, forming our self-images and making us who we are.

As mythologist Joseph Campbell said: "[Reincarnation] suggests that you are more than you think you are. There are dimensions of your being and a potential for realization and consciousness that are not included in your concept of yourself. Your life is much deeper and broader than you conceive it to be here. What you are living is but a fractional inkling of what is really within you, what gives you life, breadth, and depth. But you can live in terms of that depth. And when you can experience it, you suddenly see that all the religions are talking about that."

ANSWERS, BUT MORE QUESTIONS

My research may be helpful in that search for personal identity. Past-life regressions have certainly helped me. Through this hypnotic process, I have been able to understand why I react as I do to certain events, environments, even images. Regressions have been a valuable tool to me for added self-understanding.

But be forewarned: Like me, you may find that these experiences leave you with many questions. I don't mind that. Despite the questions, my regressions have increased my inner awareness and opened me to possibilities I hadn't dreamed of.

Another word of warning: It is easy to conclude that these vivid experiences are proof of a life before life. Although I can't prove that they aren't, I do not believe that they are. As you will see, I have come up with a simpler explanation that satisfies me. It is an explanation that you can test for yourself.

Perhaps the most interesting aspect of past-life regressions is that you can draw your own conclusions and use your regression experiences any way you wish. You can use them as valuable tools of self-discovery to reveal new solutions to old psychological conflicts, or to reach that most elusive peace of mind.

As a wise doctor said: "We are each an experiment of one. We can use the results of our research as we wish."

A few words here about how the case studies were gathered for this book: Regression hypnosis is usually a lengthy process that requires substantial questioning on the part of the therapist. In some ways it can be compared to the way in which a spouse recounts an exciting day at work. There are many questions on the part of the listener about specifics: interesting details about exact conversations that transpired, reactions to events, and descriptions of surroundings. Regression hypnosis is like that. It is an arduous series of questions and answers between subject and therapist that takes place when the subject is deeply hypnotized.

A partial transcript of one of my own patients' regressions reads like this:

> Subject: I am looking down and I can see that I am wearing a white robe.
> Therapist: Can you see other people around you?
> Subject: Yes I can.
> Therapist: What are they wearing?
> Subject: They are wearing white robes too.
> Therapist: What are they doing?
> Subject: They are standing around a stone wall in the middle of town. They all have big pots and a man is dipping a sort of bucket into a hole and pulling up water. He is filling their water pots.
> Therapist: How are the people around this well acting?
> Subject: They all appear to be happy. Something is going to happen and they are all waiting for it.

Therapist: Can you get closer to them so you can hear what they are saying?

Subject: Yes I can. I am standing with them now and I can listen to what they are saying. They are happy because the king is coming to town today. He is arriving soon because someone saw his caravan on the horizon.

And so on.

For the purposes of this book, each case study is presented as a detailed summary of the subject's experiences, related immediately following hypnosis. This process crystalized the experience for the subject as well as for me, so we could have better therapy sessions. It also provided the clear and interesting stories that are the backbone of this book.

I

—

Explorations

1

The Nine Other Lives
of Raymond Moody

My lecturing on the subject of near-death experiences has always led to questions about other extranormal phenomena. When the time comes to take questions from the audience, a good percentage of them are likely to involve things like UFO abductions, spoon bending, hauntings, and past-life regression.

Not only were all of these subjects out of my realm of study, but they were somewhat embarrassing for me. After all, none of them have anything to do with near-death experiences. To begin with, near-death experiences (NDEs) are profound spiritual events that happen, uninvited, to some individuals at the point of death. They are generally accompanied by one or more of the following symptoms: an out-of-body experience, the sense of zooming up a tunnel toward a bright light, seeing long-dead relatives at the other end of the tunnel, and having a life review that is guided by a Being of Light.

NDEs have little to do with the many other paranormal phenomena that I was frequently quizzed about after lectures. They represented other fields of study in which I had truly little interest.

That included past-life regressions. I had always presumed that these voyages back through time were a product of the subject's fantasy and nothing more. It was my guess that people daydreamed them or that they represented some bizarre kind of wish fulfillment. I assumed that most of the people who were successfully regressed found themselves to be an exotic character, such as Egyptian royalty. When asked about past lives, it was difficult for me to hide my skepticism.

I first heard about past-life regressions from Ian Stevenson, a professor at the University of Virginia. He is a psychiatrist and an expert in psychosomatic medicine who has investigated reincarnation tales gathered from around the world. Typically they are tales told by young children who spontaneously "remember" past lives.

Stevenson had at one time performed some hypnotic regressions and decided that they were very unreliable methods of looking into the question of reincarnation. He believed that the patient was reproducing something he or she had learned or heard about in years past and was now—while under hypnosis—merely projecting it outward.

There the matter stood until I met Diana Denholm. She is a lovely and persuasive psychologist who used hypnosis in her practice. Originally she used it to help people stop smoking, lose weight, and even to find lost objects. But some strange things had happened, she said. Every once in a while, a patient would start talking about experiences from a past life. Most of the time these events occurred when she took people back through their lives to recover a lost, traumatic memory, a process known as age regression therapy. This technique would help them find the source of phobias or neuroses that were creating problems. Their intent was to take a person back through their current life, layer by layer, to uncover a psychological trauma in much the way an archeologist digs through the layers of time at an archeological site to uncover relics.

The intention of regression therapy was *not* to go beyond the date on the patient's birth certificate, just far back in their current life.

But occasionally, patients would slip back even further than seemed possible. They would suddenly begin talking about another life, place, and time as though it were right there before their very eyes.

For instance, a woman who was having trouble responding to her husband's sexual needs might go to a hypnotherapist like

Denholm to see if there was any sort of forgotten abuse in her childhood that would make her sexually reticent. But in the process of regression, she might suddenly begin describing a past life in which she is a sexually abused slave girl in the roaring Roman Empire.

These were the sorts of odd things that were happening to Denholm as she conducted hypnotic regressions.

At first the experiences frightened Denholm. She thought she had done something wrong in her hypnotherapy, or perhaps she was treating someone with multiple personalities. But when this happened a few times, Denholm began to realize that she could use these experiences to help treat the patient's disorder.

With research and practice, she became quite proficient at eliciting past lives from people who would allow it. Now she uses regression therapy regularly in her practice because it frequently cuts through hours of therapy by plunging right to the heart of the problem.

What Diana had to say about regressions intrigued me. Up to that point in my life I had dismissed these experiences. But here was someone I respected, talking about a phenomenon that had not been invited, but simply happened to patients in her practice.

Believing that each of us is an experiment of one, I wanted to experience past-life regressions myself. I expressed my desire to Diana, who graciously offered to do a regression that very afternoon. She seated me in an overstuffed recliner and led me, slowly and skillfully, into a deep trance. Later she said I had been under for about an hour. At all times I was aware of being Raymond Moody and of being under the guidance of a wonderful hypnotist. But at the same time I went back through nine civilizations and was able to see myself and the world in many different incarnations. To this day I don't know what they meant—or even if they meant anything. I do know that they were very intense experiences, more like reality than a dream. The colors were as real as life and the events unfolded from their own inner logic and not through any "wishing" of my own. I was not saying, "What do I want to happen next?" or "How should the plot go?" These vivid lives just happened of their own accord, like movies on a screen.

A couple of general notes about the lives I passed through in this fascinating voyage of the mind: Only two of them took place during time periods that I could recognize, both in ancient Rome. The others gave no evidence by which I could date them in terms of modern Western history. They were either prehistoric, in primitive societies, or had no historic context at all.

When I began to see these episodes they had such a familiarity that they were drenched with nostalgia. It was truly as though I was remembering actual experiences. Some were fragmentary; others were so complete and real that I felt as though I was remembering my own life by watching family films.

Here, in chronological order, is the series of lives through which I passed with Diana Denholm's guidance.

LIFETIME #1: JUNGLE LIFE

In the first incarnation, I was a proto-human, some prehistoric version of man. Definitely an arboreal creature, I lived high in the trees in the comfort of branches and leaves. I was surprisingly manlike; certainly not an ape.

I wasn't alone, but was with a group of beings living together in nestlike structures. We helped each other construct these homes and made certain that we had access to one another. Not only did we know that there was safety in numbers, we also knew there was comfort in numbers. We must have been fairly far along in the scale of the brain's evolution. Although I was this apelike creature, I had an appreciation of beauty. I know this because we chose a pretty place to live, as though our surroundings were a priority for us. Flowers in hues of pink that carpeted the tops of the trees were all around our living platform and provided wonderful natural decorations, a veritable sea of colors.

My center of gravity was in my shoulders during this experience, unlike the way humans are now, where our center of gravity is in our hips. I moved around in a bent-over fashion with my arms dangling near my feet. I could stand with some difficulty, but usually I moved on all fours when I needed speed and agility.

I remember a great sense of curiosity as well as fear about

life down there on the ground. At one point an animal that looked like a wild boar ran beneath our tree, making a terrible ruckus. I remember this upsetting me and my fellow "pre-humans." That led to another strange new feeling: The fear we felt was a frenetic, disorganizing kind of fear that made us want to jump up and down in a frenzy. Yet mixed with it there was a strong curiosity. I wanted very much to get a closer look at that animal, almost to the point of letting this curiosity overcome good sense.

While having these feelings of almost fatal curiosity, I realized that I was unable to express myself verbally. Our method of communication was merely to let our emotions show. Instead of talking, we were left with the frustration of acting out our needs and feelings through pantomime.

I also remember that we were fruit eaters. I vividly recall eating a fruit that I didn't recognize. It was juicy and full of red seeds. It was so completely real to me that I actually had the sense of eating it right there in hypnosis. I could even feel the juice running down my chin as I crunched the fruit in my mouth.

During my regression, I had no control over when I passed out of each remembered lifetime. My subconscious mind seemed to select for me what I should see, fading one scene out and another in. So I had a little glimpse of my life in the trees and then I went on to another life.

LIFETIME #2: PRIMITIVE AFRICA

In this life, I was about twelve years of age, living with a group of people in a tropical forest in a land of spectacular beauty. I gather from the fact that all of us were black that this was Africa.

At the beginning of this hypnotic adventure, I found myself in the woods looking down a gradual slope to a stark white strip of beach on the shore of a calm lake. There was thin tropical forest all around the village that became denser as it moved up the hills, away from the village, and into the mountains.

The houses we lived in were about two feet off the ground on stout poles. The walls were made of woven straw that surrounded a large square room. I couldn't tell much more about the place except that it was very comfortable. The weather was balmy and the breeze from the lake kept the air fresh inside the huts.

I went on to see random scenes from this life.

At one point I was a little boy fishing on the shores of the lake. The men were out on the water in boats, but I was too young to be allowed to join them. Still I was proud of my contribution to the village food supply, a string of fish I caught on my own. I planned to stay out there in the shallows casting my net and hauling in fish until sundown.

Although I never saw my parents in this episode, I had a strong sense of their presence. For instance, I knew my father was out in one of those boats working with the other men of the village and that my mother was with the women, but I never saw them. I was simply aware of the comfort of their nearness.

At another point when I was older, I was journeying up an incredibly rugged blue/black mountain. We were hiking barefoot up a primitive trail, carrying long spears and wooden shields that were brightly painted with images of animals.

All of us were brightly decorated with war paint. Although the path was very steep and tough to climb, we held our breathing to a quiet minimum to avoid making too much noise.

The great feeling of fear that I had made me think that we were going into battle. I remember being very tired and frightened. I didn't understand why I was on this trip and I had a deep longing to return to my home by the lake.

Then this life faded.

LIFETIME #3: THE MASTER BOAT BUILDER STUMBLES

In my next episode, I saw myself from a third-person vantage point as a very old, muscular man. I had blue eyes, long silver hair, and was still—at this late age—laboring hard at my profession as a master boat builder.

I was working in a long building that was entirely open on one side, which faced a large river. In the building there were long beams and heavy pieces of wood. On the walls and strewn about the ground were the primitive tools of the boat builder's trade.

These were to be the final hours of my life. With me was my granddaughter who was about three years old and very timid. I was talking to her, demonstrating the various tools on a boat that I had just completed while she timidly peeked over the boat's gunwales.

That day I launched the boat and took my granddaughter out for a pleasure trip. We were enjoying ourselves on the placid river when a wall of water suddenly came rushing over us and the boat was engulfed. I was thrown one way and I saw my granddaughter being swept the other way. I thrashed about in the water, trying hard to reach her, but nature was faster and stronger than I. Sadly I watched her being sucked under.

At that point I gave up. I remember going under for the last time with a great sense of guilt over having instigated the boat trip that killed my sweet little granddaughter.

In my hypnotic state the fear was as vivid as though I was really drowning. My heart pounded and my blood pressure rose as I heard the water rushing around my ears and sensed the struggle of trying to get hold of the boat. My hands slipped from the wooden boat and the water gagged me as I went under. I went down feeling all the guilt that a grandparent would have about being responsible for the death of a grandchild. This guilt changed to ecstasy as I neared death. At that point a bright light engulfed me and I was overcome with total bliss. I knew at that point that everything would be all right for both my granddaughter and myself. It was truly a feeling of relief.

LIFETIME #4: THE FEARFUL MAMMOTH HUNTER

In the next life I found myself a member of a band of people who were desperately hunting woolly mammoth.

It is not my usual style to take on something so big, least of all a woolly mammoth. But in my hypnotic state I could see we were not a well-fed group of people and truly needed the food.

We were dressed in animal skins that left us barely warm enough for survival. They covered our chests and shoulders, but did little to protect us from the cold and nothing to conceal our private parts. Not that either of those factors mattered at the time, since we were thinking little about warmth or decorum while fighting this mammoth. Six of us were down in a little gully hitting this powerful animal with rocks and sticks.

The mammoth grabbed one of the tribe members with its trunk and with a clean, efficient move, simply crushed his head. It was a primeval horror.

In the midst of this horror I remember thinking that there must be a better way of getting food than this. To say that it was a nerve-racking and depressing experience is to understate this dramatic memory.

But it was also one that afforded some helpful perspectives. I was able to view this not only from the first-person perspective of a participant, but also in the third person, like watching a movie on a screen. This perspective was somewhat confusing to me. It was as though I suddenly had an out-of-body experience and was able to view myself in an intense activity.

LIFETIME #5: EARLY PUBLIC WORKS

Luckily I moved on. This time I found myself in the midst of an enormous public-works project at a time that I assumed was near the dawn of civilization. I was not a king in this dream or even a job foreman, but simply one of the workers. I think we were working on an aqueduct or a road system, but I'm not sure, since I couldn't see the center of activity from where I was.

We workers lived in rows of white stone apartment buildings with little parks between them. I lived in an upstairs apartment with my wife and had the sense that we had lived there for years, because the place felt very familiar.

The room we lived in had a little sleeping platform that my wife and I were lying on. I was extremely hungry and my wife was quite literally dying of starvation. She just lay on the bed looking very gaunt and waiting for her life to flicker out. We lay quietly, trying to conserve energy to survive another day. In my regression I could see her: fatless, muscleless, and too tired to even flicker a smile. Hunger had aged her, but she was probably about forty years old, with charcoal black hair and a high-cheekboned face.

I had the feeling that we'd had a good life together, but the lack of food dulled many memories.

We weren't alone in our hunger. There must have been a famine going on because the whole of society was starving. All of the men I worked with were tired and hungry first thing every morning. I remember struggling up a hill to go to work in the morning. None of us talked because we didn't have the energy. We just trudged on silently.

I had a great sense of guilt because my wife was dying and I could do nothing to protect her.

I remember walking somberly up that hill, looking back at our apartment and feeling very forlorn. Then this life faded out.

LIFETIME #6: THROWN TO THE LIONS

In the next lifetime, I was finally in a culture that I recognized—ancient Rome. Unfortunately I was neither an emperor nor a nobleman. I found myself in a lion's pit, about to be devoured as a public amusement.

Briefly, I saw myself in the third person. I had long, reddish-brown hair and a mustache. I was very thin and wore only a pair of leather shorts. I knew something of my personal history. I knew that I was from an area now known as Germany and had been captured during one of the military campaigns of the Roman Empire. I had been used by the army to carry booty back to Rome and was now about to be put to death solely for the Romans' amusement. I could see myself looking up at a crowd of people surrounding the top of the pit. I must have been looking to them for mercy because behind the gate beside me was a desperately hungry lion. I could feel its energy and hear the noise it made as it prepared to devour me.

I knew there was no escape, yet when the gate was raised, my survival instincts took over and I began to look for a way out. My visual perspective changed and I was now inside my body looking out. Quickly I looked up to the right and then to the left. As I looked to the left, my eyes caught those of a spectator. He looked like the most evil man I have ever seen, devoid of emotion or kindness. His hair was long, brown, and closely cropped on top of his round head. His left eye was pink and infected, creating an even more emotionless look on his face.

He was sitting next to an obese character who was wearing a dirty toga. He wasn't paying any particular attention to me, but the fellow with pinkeye was staring at me as he put a snack in his mouth. When our eyes met, he just chuckled and chewed. He didn't even appear to be so informed as to be sadistic. My death was just an amusement for him.

What happened next was a blur. I heard the latch slide back on the gate and saw the lion push it open and lunge for me. I tried to protect myself by holding my arms up but the lion came like they weren't even there. To the roaring delight of the crowd I was slammed to the ground and pinned down by the animal.

The last thing I remember was being held between a pair of paws, about to have my skull crushed by the lion's powerful jaws. I assume that the next sound I would have heard would have been the crunching of my skull. Mercifully I was spared that sound as this life faded away.

LIFETIME #7: NOBILITY TO THE END

My next life *was* one of nobility, and again it was in ancient Rome.

I was in a beautiful apartment that glowed with the fading light of early evening and the yellow light of several oil lamps that gave the marble walls of the room a glistening luster.

I was wearing a white toga and lying on a sofa shaped like a modern-day chaise longue. I think I was in my forties and had a slight potbelly and the soft skin of a bureaucrat who doesn't do much hard labor. I remember a feeling of complete complacency as I lay there looking at my son. He appeared to be about fifteen and had hair that was wavy, dark, and closely cut, beautifully framing his frightened face.

He said, "Father, why are those people trying to get in here?"

Even though terror filled his face, I was totally complacent. I continued to lie on this couch with my hands behind my head, propping it up so I could see my terrified son. "Why, son," I said. "That's why we have the soldiers."

"But, father, there are so many of them," he said. He looked so frightened that I decided to get up out of idle curiosity just to see what he was talking about. I walked over to the balcony and saw a handful of Roman soldiers pushing back a huge mob of disgruntled people.

At that point I knew there was good reason to be as frightened as my son. I looked at my son and knew from his response that all the fear I suddenly experienced had registered on my face.

That was the end of that lifetime. From the feelings I had after seeing the crowd, I think that my life was almost over anyway.

LIFETIME #8: DEATH IN THE DESERT

The next life took me to a mountainous area somewhere in the deserts of the Middle East. I was a merchant with a house up the hill from my store.

My place of business was a tiny stall where I bought and sold jewelry. I would sit there all day and appraise gold, silver, and precious stones. In some cases I sold the work of metalsmiths. I also traded with caravans that passed by on this trade route. Although this place didn't look like much, it was well-known that I made a lot of money.

My home was my pride. It was a wonderful reddish-brick place with a porch situated in such a way that the cool evening air made it a perfect place to while away the time. The house was pressed against a mountain and as a result had no back yard, only a view of distant mountains and river valleys that gave this desert region its interesting terrain. The house itself had a large living room with a stone floor and open pillared archways providing a view as well as good airflow when there was a breeze.

I remembered taking long, relaxing walks through the hills with my wife to watch the sun sink and turn the sky red.

One day I came home and had a sense as I approached that all was strangely quiet. I went inside and passed from silent room to silent room, feeling the fear intensify. Then I went into our bedroom and found my wife and three young children dead, brutally murdered. I am not sure how they were killed, but from the amount of blood my guess was that they were hacked apart with knives.

I knew from the feeling I had under hypnosis that this was a tragedy from which I never recovered. I don't know where my physical life ended in that incarnation, but I do know that life was essentially over with that horrible event.

LIFETIME #9: THE ORIENTAL ARTIST

In the final lifetime of my regression hypnosis I found myself as a Chinese artist. A *woman* artist.

The first event I remember was that I was a little girl of about six and I had a younger brother. Our parents had taken us to a beautiful spot similar in grandeur to a place like Yosemite Falls. There were paths leading up to spectacular walls of granite that had waterfalls pouring from open cracks in the walls. We stood in one spot, looking up at a cascading waterfall that fell past us and into a deep crevasse. Although there was a guardrail, I was afraid that my little brother was going to fall down into this abyss. I was very concerned about him and kept a tight hold on his arm. My childish concern was a source of amusement for my parents, who were both looking down and laughing at me.

I moved forward to later ages and could see that my life was devoted to art. There were several scenes in which I could see myself painting. In some of these I could see my work from the perspective of the canvas. I could see how my strokes went on and how each of them had meaning within the whole picture.

My studio was airy and lighted by a large window. I was

about thirty years old at this point in my life and I had a stooped shape, perhaps from a birth defect or a dietary deficiency.

This regression contained several fragmentary memories.

At one point I remembered being downtown in the village where I lived and meeting an old friend. We were talking on the sidewalk when suddenly, in the middle of the street, an intense flash of light appeared. We were both puzzled as to what this phenomenon had been. It was brilliant, like a magnesium flash.

We were baffled by what we saw. We went to a known wise man, a philosopher, to find the explanation for this vision. He had none, other than to tell us of a similar incident that had occurred several years before in another town.

At another point in this life I went to a large stone house to visit an elderly aunt. She seemed to be in her sixties and was beaming with joy at seeing me, her favorite niece. Her gray hair was pulled back and tied in a braid. I could see her very clearly, standing on her porch in cotton pants and a shirt, looking down at me and talking as I came up the stairs.

Those were brief images. Then I went forward to the point of my death. I had become impoverished and was living in a tiny house located in an alleyway behind some wealthy homes. It was comfortable. I had a bed and a stove and a window that gave me enough light to do my painting. But despite the location, the area wasn't safe. I was lying there asleep on this last day of my life, when a young man came in and strangled me. It was just that simple. He didn't take any of my possessions. He only wanted the one thing that had no value to him, my life.

As I died, I rose above my body and had no concern for me, the victim. My concern was for the young murderer, who was standing above the body in sort of a cocky pose, clearly proud of his work. I was trying to ask the young man why he had done this to me. I wanted to know what had made him so unhappy that he thought he had to kill an old woman.

I waved at him, shouted, but he couldn't see me. There was no way I could communicate with him. Finally I just seemed to fade away, out of that life. To where, I do not know.

·   ·   ·

That was it. Nine lifetimes and one hour later, I had a new, entirely changed perspective on these "things" called past-life regressions. Diana Denholm brought me slowly out of the hypnotic trance. She was obviously amused at the perplexed look on my face because she was smiling broadly when I opened my eyes and looked at her.

"Amazing, isn't it," she said.

I completely agreed. I realized that my assumptions about past-life regressions had been wrong. The images I had experienced had nothing to do with wish fulfillment. After all, when had I ever wished to fight a woolly mammoth or be eaten by a lion as part of a public spectacle? There was clearly something going on here. Do these past-life regressions really tap past lives or just the fantasy world of our subconscious? "It depends upon your point of view," said Denholm. She was clearly amused at my puzzlement. So was I. And I was a little embarrassed. All these years I had rejected the notion of past-life regressions, considering them some kind of hocus-pocus. Now that I'd had one, what was I going to do?

I began making mental notes.

On the surface, it seemed that past-life regressions took place at a unique level of consciousness, one that had its own distinct features. They were not like dreams, nor were they like daydreams. These experiences had a feeling of familiarity to them. As they unfolded, I seemed to be remembering them rather than making them up.

However, they afforded something that real experience doesn't. While in a regression state, I was able to see myself from various perspectives. So, for instance, I was above myself for part of that horrifying time in the lion pit, watching the action as though I were a spectator. But I was also in the pit. The same was true when I flashed back to my days as a boat builder. For a while I watched myself build that boat from a third-person perspective. Then, for seemingly no reason and with no ability to control the situation, I was back in my body viewing the world from the point of view of the old boat builder.

This change in perspective was mysterious. But so were other things. From where were these "visions" coming? At the time, I had no interest whatsoever in history. Yet here I was, drifting through different historical periods, some that I knew and some that I didn't. Were they real or were they conjured?

I knew from my experience as a physician and psychiatrist that I couldn't jump to conclusions about these vivid experiences. On the surface they certainly seemed to be proof of reincarnation. But being a psychiatrist, I know that the mind is a deep and wondrous thing, an organ that functions on many levels. At its least obvious level, it can be a random gatherer of information and images, bits of information that stick in the mind for seemingly no reason.

Sitting in Diana's Florida living room, I recalled one such instance. A psychotherapist friend once reported his experience with a "past life" to me. He was hypnotized and told to go back to a past life. Surprisingly one came to mind. He found himself wandering through rock dwellings in what seemed to be the deserts of the southwestern United States. He saw in vivid detail the insides of round-roomed sanctuaries of the most sacred spots. He was even able to describe the clothing his people wore and some of the tools they fashioned for agricultural cultivation.

It wasn't until several months later at his parents' home that he was watching some scratchy home movies of childhood vacations and found himself watching the very scenes that had been recalled by past-life hypnosis! He had merely tapped a childhood memory.

Still I couldn't discount the possibility of reincarnation. Besides not wanting to declare that millions of Hindus are wrong, there were many unexplainable regressions that had come to my attention.

My own past-life regression confused me. I didn't truly expect to experience past lives while under hypnosis. If I did see something, I didn't think the experience would be so unexplicable. If anything, I thought I would find myself in a previous life as the outlaw Jesse James because of some book I had read, or Julius Caesar from my memory of a movie. But the nine lives that I experienced under hypnosis were very much a surprise. Most of them appeared to be during times I had never even read about, let alone seen in movies. And I was essentially an average person in each of them, which for me shot down the theory that everyone who goes into a past life sees himself as Cleopatra or some similarly glamorous historical figure.

A few days after my regression I admitted that the experience was now a mystery to me. The only way I could begin to unravel this mystery was to structure a scientific study that would examine regressions, taking them apart and looking at their component parts. I hoped to do with past-life regressions what I had done with near-death experiences: analyze them for their common elements to see how one regression experience could be compared to another.

I jotted down some of the questions I hoped to answer in my exploration of past-life regressions:

✳ Can medical conditions, both mental and physical, be affected by past-life therapy?

The mind/body connection is a subject being deeply considered these days, yet little work has been done on the effects of regressions on medical problems.

I was especially interested in the effect this therapy might have on phobias, those unexplained fears that people often have. I had heard that regressions were often able to reveal the root cause of these fears, enabling the person to overcome the problem. Now I would examine that question for myself.

✳ How can these strange journeys be explained? If one doesn't believe that these occurrences are proof of reincarnation, how can they be explained?

At this time I didn't have an answer. But I began jotting down some possible explanations. One was that the mind creates its own dramas, almost like self-created television programs. These dramas exist at that unconscious level that Jung claims is so active in each of us. These past lives, I thought, are almost like personal myths in each of us.

I began looking for research to provide back-up to this theory.

✳ Yet, how can we explain the truly mysterious cases?

Although I didn't necessarily believe that these are proof of reincarnation as so many people do, I must admit that some of the cases I'd heard couldn't be explained away very easily.

✳ Can people tap their own past lives, without using a hypnotist?

I wanted to know if self-hypnosis can be as effective as hypnotherapy in experiencing these past lives.

On the airplane home, I realized that I had allowed Diana Denholm to hypnotize me in hopes of garnering some answers from the experience. The results had been quite the opposite. Now I was filled with questions that had to be answered. My curiosity was piqued. I was now ready to explore past lives.

2

Traits of
Past-Life Regressions

I began my research at home.

I was teaching psychology at Western Georgia State College in Carrollton, and despite the conservative air of this traditional southern town (a large marble sculpture of a Confederate soldier occupies a prominent place near city center), Western Georgia State has a psychology department that emphasizes the study of the paranormal. This emphasis is rare in modern colleges and universities. Most of the psychology departments in the U.S. have gone the way of mainstream psychology itself, which prefers to employ cognitive therapy. Linked mainly with behaviorism, cognitive therapy limits itself to types of therapy and experience that can be empirically proven.

Western Georgia doesn't ignore cognitive therapy, and it offers many courses that keep students well within the mainstream. But when William Roll, Director of the Psychical Research Foundation, joined the psychology department in the eighties, he wanted to be sure that the many paranormal phenomena that occur would also be dealt with in their fascinating depth. Although many of these are state-induced phenomena and can't be controlled or created in a laboratory setting, the founding fathers of this department wanted to make certain that the students knew about the unexplained as well as the contrivable and controllable.

That is why you'll find courses on ghosts, near-death experiences, and astrology mixed with courses on hypnosis and self-hypnosis and modern-day shamanic psychotherapy.

TRAITS OF REGRESSIONS

My first step in past-life research was to hypnotize a large number of people and try to lead them into past-life regressions in order to examine the qualities of the experience. The people I planned to use were students in my classes. The goal of this research was to uncover the traits of past-life regressions so they could be better understood and used by therapists.

I had accomplished this same goal in the early seventies with the near-death experience. By dissecting the near-death experiences of about two hundred people I had revealed the common threads that define that spiritual experience. The eleven common traits in NDEs gave therapists, doctors, and patients themselves a guide to understanding these puzzling events.

For my past-life research I needed about fifty people who were willing experimental subjects. They had to be compliant and open to new experiences. They had to have flexible hours and be willing to spend more than the planned time if some of the regressions ran longer than expected. These requirements made students the perfect study group. I put the word out in the psychology department and was soon able to enlist more than fifty ready, willing, and able subjects.

I planned to try a variety of regression techniques with them. The main emphasis would be on individual regressions, in which the subjects would be brought into my office and we would conduct the hypnotism session one-on-one.

Not wanting to limit myself to a student population, I also performed many individual regressions with people in the general population to account for any bias that might be found in just using students.

I expected the best results from individual regressions. People tend to hypnotize more deeply when they are alone. Still I wanted to try some group sessions just to see what the results would be. As it turned out, the lives "recalled" weren't as complete or colorful as the individual regressions, but I did encounter one interesting extrasensory phenomenon: On several occasions a student on one side of the class would experience virtually the same past life as a student on the other side. For instance, a woman who described herself as a ballet dancer wearing blue tights and dancing in front of a large audience on a brightly lighted stage was describing practically the same experience as that of a woman on the other side of the room.

The third type of regression technique that I planned to experiment with was the lost art of scrying, better known as crystal-ball gazing.

Very popular among Tibetan wise men and the spiritually enlightened of other countries, scrying was even used by the Queen of England to provide personal guidance through the morass of state affairs that she had to deal with. In this technique the subject literally gazes into a crystal ball or some other clear depth while being hypnotically induced.

I used the crystal-ball technique both in groups and with individuals. Overall, it gave the best results of all, perhaps because the crystal ball gave the subject a sense of control.

REGRESSION THERAPISTS

I decided that my own regressions weren't enough. I needed some outside resources with which to compare my findings.

I found case studies I needed in the files of several psychologists specializing in the growing field of regression therapy.

This cutting-edge "New Age" therapy first became the focus of an official association in the spring of 1980. According to Hazel Denning, a noted regression therapist, fifty-two therapists met in a private session in Irvine, California, to start an association for past-life therapists. The purpose of the association was to provide a central clearinghouse for past-life information and training.

Now the Association for Past-Life Research and Therapy has several hundred members worldwide. They have a very active conference and workshop schedule and even publish a bi-annual research journal and a quarterly newsletter.

Past-life therapists believe that past-life experiences can affect a person's current outlook and behavior. So, for instance, a person who fears fire might do so because a past-life experience had them burning to death in Rome while Nero fiddled. Or they may fear airplane travel because a past-life experience finds them as a passenger on the ill-fated Hindenberg.

Past-life regression therapists readily admit to being outside the mainstream of psychology. Nonetheless, they are proud of this exploration into a brave new world, unrestrained by the shackles of empiricism.

In the first issue of *The Journal of Regression Therapy*, editor Irene Hickman proclaimed:

> The members of the APRT [use] techniques that uncover and reveal happenings from the past—sometimes from long distant past—which are causing present illness, disharmony or malfunction. We have found within our own experience that when a patient or client has a problem of any kind, there is a cause, that this cause can be elicited using regression techniques, that the cause can be so treated as to neutralize the effect, allowing a return to health.
>
> We admit that neither our research nor our therapy fits exactly into the scientific mold. Perhaps this arises from the strict limitations of science—so strict that no experimentation with human subjects can be made to fit the scientific paradigm requiring exact repeatability.
>
> Since no experiments using human subjects can be repeated exactly, perhaps it will become necessary for Science to postulate a new paradigm. Lacking this wider view, Science excludes research that could reveal the true nature of the human mind, the nature of consciousness, and answer the question of survival after bodily death.
>
> We are convinced that we have found and are continuing to find answers that are important to the family of man. We will enhance understanding, enable the development of greater health, harmony, inner peace and creativity. The techniques we use are helping our patients/clients reach their optimum creativity.

Surprisingly, past-life regression therapists don't necessarily believe in past lives, just the experience. It isn't unusual to hear them refer to regressions as "fantasies," or to draw the distinction between "authentic regressions" and "metaphorical dream states."

In a paper published in the journal, therapist Garrett Oppenheim tells of a woman who is raped in her life as a seventeenth-century farm girl. According to his account, she was feeding the pigs when she was abducted by four strangers who threw her into the pigsty, beat her, and raped her repeatedly. When they had their fill of her, they pushed her face into the muck and suffocated her.

Later, when he asked her what the regressions meant, she blurted out, "I'm not going to be afraid of sex with my husband anymore."

As Oppenheim wrote it:

> Her husband, she reported in class the next week, didn't dig all this nonsense about reincarnation. I carefully emphasized to her—and to the whole class—that it didn't matter whether a reincarnation experience was literally true or not. What did matter was the therapeutic results. The following week, Doris announced that both she and her husband had to agree with me—"Wholeheartedly."

The therapists I contacted did believe in past lives. They were convinced through personal experience and those that they elicited in their patients that memory survived death and was deeply buried in our minds. "Given the chance," said one of the therapists, "I could help you glimpse something—even a fragment —of every one of your lives."

From the looks of the files that she and the other therapists let me see, they had done that very thing with several people.

Many of the clients had experienced several lives under the care of these skillful hypnotists. Some had been just like mine, vivid events that seemed to be connected to nothing in particular. Others were far more detailed and filled with meaning relating to the patient's present life.

But whether the past-life experience was intricate in its detail or sketchy and fragmentary, each contained certain identifiable traits. By analyzing my research and the files of the regression therapists I was able to isolate twelve traits present with past-life regressions.

I am not saying that a person isn't having a regression experience if they don't have all of the dozen traits outlined below. I am saying, however, that they can expect several of these "symptoms" when undergoing past-life regressions.

Trait #1: Past-Life Experiences Are Usually Visual

Most of my subjects say that their past-life experiences consist largely of sensory images. These images are usually visual, but in a few cases odors and sounds are also described. The subjects say the images are more vivid or "real" than those in ordinary daydreams. Usually they do not seem distorted in the bizarre ways familiar to us from the dreams we normally have.

The past-life images are usually described as being in color, as well. Here is one such example from a woman who was regressed and found herself as a farm boy in the late 1800s.

> I was an eighteen-year-old boy, sitting on the back of a wagon with my feet dangling down. I was right there. I could see my feet hanging down off the back of the wagon as clearly as if I had done it only five minutes ago.
>
> Later in the same life, I was out working on a fence and I could see a snake at my feet just as plain as if it were right here in front of us. I ran to get away from it and fell and hit my forehead on a rock. The pain was so vivid that I had a headache when I came out of the trance. I also thought that blood was dripping down my face even after I came out of hypnosis because I could still feel it from the rock that caused me to bleed in my trance.

This is just one example of the way the senses are stimulated by past-life regressions.

Less often, a past-life experience takes place in the form of thoughts. Not surprisingly, people whose past-life experiences are devoid of imagery are usually those who claim they have very little mental imagery in their "current" day-to-day inner life. However, this lack of sensory images doesn't make the experience any less compelling. Regressions that consist only of thoughts can be as moving and captivating as those comprised of vivid and vibrant imagery.

Trait #2: Past-Life Regressions Seem to Have a Life of Their Own

The scenes and events visualized during a past-life encounter seem to unfold of their own accord, as though their outcome and progression were somehow independent of the conscious control of the person undergoing the experience. As a result, subjects usually feel as if they are witnessing events, not making them up like a daydreamer would. Subjects frequently describe the feeling as that of watching a movie that seems somewhat familiar.

A good example is my own regression. When I found myself as the Chinese lady artist I was not sitting there making decisions about what would happen next. I had the feeling that I was just sitting there watching a movie. The events unfolded scene by scene. For me it was just like watching the big screen. Everything was in vivid color and detail. All I had to do was sit there and watch.

Trait #3: The Imagery Has an Uncanny Feeling of Familiarity

The past-life encounter is often permeated with a sense of familiarity, even nostalgia. The feelings these people have are very similar to the common experience of déjà vu, the feeling that one has already done or seen whatever he or she is currently experiencing.

These feelings of familiarity may range in intensity from a vague sense of remembrance to seeming to suddenly remember the events, once long forgotten, but now forcefully recaptured.

One such example is the regression of a patient we'll call Neal. This Georgian who was raised Southern Baptist went to the unlikely lifetime of that of a monk in Ireland. He had many experiences that were steeped in familiarity, but perhaps the most vivid was when he and another monk watched from the top of a hill as some elderly farmers were murdered by thieves.

> It was horrifying, but very much like I had seen it before. We had just topped the hill and were looking down at this farm when we noticed a band of horsemen riding toward the farmhouse. The old farmer and his wife came out to see who was coming and these horsemen rode right up to them and hit them with swords and clubs. We then watched as they dismounted and began ransacking the house.
>
> When I saw this in my trance, it didn't surprise me. I had this feeling of "Oh yeah. I remember that." It was horrible. But I had been there before.

Sometimes the experience awakens a feeling of homesickness for the apparent previous life. The subject may even come away drenched with nostalgia for the lost world.

One of my patients went back to ancient China in his regression and was able to visit with his mentor, an old sage who had taught him well throughout the years of this previous life. Now he likes to come in for regressions just so he can visit with that old man!

Trait #4: The Subject Identifies with One Character

A person undergoing a past-life regression identifies himself as one of the individuals in the unfolding drama. The subject maintains this uncanny sense of being that person despite what may be profound differences in physical appearance, life circumstances, occupation, sex, or a host of other factors.

For example, one of the students in my college class reported with all apparent sincerity and conviction that he was a merchant living in Turkey hundreds of years ago.

In another regression, a young Southern housewife described her sense of having actually been an African warrior in the dim primeval past.

I suddenly found myself as a black warrior dressed in nothing but some kind of grass skirt to cover my privates! My jet black skin was covered with very elaborate patterns of war paint that zig-zagged all over my body and made me look extremely fierce.

I now realize the purpose of the war paint. It may seem silly to us now, but when I was in my regression I found myself looking into the eyes of this man coming up against me in warfare. He had war paint on and the paint helped strike terror into my heart! The purpose of the paint was to add to the emotional impact of hand-to-hand combat!

This identity may linger even into the posthypnotic period. The subject may come away feeling quite sure that he or she actually was that person in a past life.

Trait #5: Past-Life Emotions May Be (Re)experienced During a Regression

Subjects usually report that they feel the emotions of their character in the regression. Thus, in one of my own regressions, I actually felt some (mercifully not all) of the terrible terror as a lion leaped on me in the closing moments of my life there in the Roman Coliseum.

This emotional "reliving" is also quite apparent to the hypnotist conducting the regression. The subject may scowl with anger upon "reliving" an event which made the person in the regression furious. Tears may flow copiously as a subject, seemingly "back in time," experiences a particularly touching or sad episode. The entire gamut of human feelings from tender love to fury may come to the surface during a deep past-life regression.

The emotions may be so powerful that it is sometimes helpful for the hypnotist to reassure the subject that he or she had "lived through" the experience in a lifetime long ago, that there is no reason to fear or be distressed by the situation anymore.

Trait #6: Past-Life Events May Be Viewed in Two Distinct Perspectives: First and Third-Person

A person undergoing a past-life regression may have a bilocality of perspective enabling him to (re)view the events from a first-person perspective (the perspective you have in day-to-day living) or a third-person perspective, in which the subject becomes a "disembodied" observer, viewing the action from outside the body of the person with whom they identify.

For example, a young student of mine described a scene from her regression in which she believed she was a coachman in early nineteenth-century Europe. At one point in the drama, she saw the action from the point of view of the coachman himself. She seemed to be in his body, viewing the road in front of him from his perch on the top of the coach. She saw the horses racing forward and even felt the wind. Then there was an accident, the coach overturned. Suddenly, she found herself viewing the scene from above looking at the coachman's twisted body in the wreckage below.

Another example comes from a snippet of a patient's regression.

> I saw a man walking along the road in a blousy outfit like the ones they wore in the Renaissance. I found that I could watch the action from above this man as well as from his perspective. I could switch perspectives at will, almost like a TV station can switch cameras to change points of view.

Trait #7: The Experience Often Mirrors Present Issues in the Subject's Life

In most of the past-life regressions I have conducted, the events and situations that unfold reflect the dilemmas and conflicts faced by the subject in his or her present life. Usually, these connections are very obvious.

For example, a patient I was working with was involved in a stressful relationship with a somewhat older woman who was attempting to dominate him. The results left him feeling helpless.

When he was hypnotized, a past life unfolded in which he had been a slave girl in an ancient Middle-Eastern city.

I remember being in a very beautiful palace in a place that seemed to be rows of apartments where slaves were coming in and out taking care of these beautiful women. I was one of them, the kept flock. We were kept as concubines for someone, a sultan perhaps.

On one hand it was great there because we were completely comfortable with all of our material needs taken care of. On the other hand it was the worst sort of hell because we had no inner freedom.

This regression was intriguing to me because he was a subjugated woman. Why? I wondered. After further therapy sessions I was able to conclude that to him, all women were in a form of subjugation. And, since his current girlfriend had subjugated him, he was feeling like a woman.

The relationship of his past-life experience to his present life's circumstance became quite clear.

But while the similarity is plain to an observer, it might not be so clear to the subject. This comes as no surprise to me. We humans routinely blind ourselves to even the most pervasive hang-ups by relegating them to our unconscious minds.

Some subjects don't need the similarities between these past lives and their current ones pointed out. Many people awaken from the hypnotic trance with the full insight that the past-life experience they just had was very similar to their present-life problems.

This tendency for past-life memories to echo current circumstances sometimes leads people to wonder whether their present difficulties result from unresolved problems in a past life.

That the regression experience is so similar to one's current affairs is part of the rationale for what is called past-life therapy. We will discuss this subject more fully later, but for now it can be pointed out that the hypnotist may be able to use regression experiences as a window into the subject's present troubles.

Trait #8: Regression May Be Followed by Genuine Improvement in Mental State

Catharsis is a psychological process in which pent-up feelings are finally allowed to be expressed, resulting in an enormous feeling of release and relief. This process often permits people to arrive at a new perspective on a sticky conflict, or to make a needed change in a stressful or debilitating relationship.

Catharsis of this kind often occurs during a past-life regression, as in the case of a young man who was locked in bitter resentment toward his younger brother, whom he saw as taking all the resources and attention of his parents. During his past-life regression, the young man witnessed a previous life in which he had lived in a jungle, apparently in South America, as an old man who was a member of a native tribe.

In that life, there was an elderly woman who the subject identified as his present-life brother. The elderly woman didn't look like his present brother. He made the connection through intuition—he "sensed" that this person in the regression was his brother.

In this regression scenario, the old man (the patient) was deformed and relied entirely upon the old woman (his current brother) for his livelihood. She had, in essence, sacrificed herself for him.

The subject emerged from the past-life regression with a new feeling of love for his brother. He now felt that the balance was being restored. In a past life his brother had graciously borne his burden. Now it was his turn to care for his brother.

As a result of this past-life regression, the subject told his younger brother of his feelings, and their relationship reached a new and more satisfying equilibrium.

All of my patients have had some point in their regression that intersects with one of the plaguing problems in their life. It might not be very dramatic in some cases, but they all say, "Since that regression I understand more about . . ."

One patient who had such catharsis from a regression is a woman I'll call Vicky. Her parents split up when she was two and she never knew her father. Although her step-father was not a strict disciplinarian, Vicky resented his authority. Because there were no blood ties, Vicky thought he should have no say in the way she was raised.

Her attitudes toward her step-father changed after her regression. In that experience, Vicky found her role switched with that of her step-father. Through a single regression, she was better able to understand his point of view.

> I was on the coast of North Africa where I found myself as a man. I had been saddled with the difficult task of raising my brother's children because he had died and there was nowhere else for his children to go. I was very poor in this lifetime, which made it a great struggle to properly take care of all of these children. . .
>
> . . . At the end of this life I found myself an old man in a mud hut. As I was dying I was surrounded by all of the children. The thing that came back to me as I died was that I had been so embroiled in supporting these children—and resented it so much—that I had not really gotten to know them as people. I felt very sad that I hadn't paid them more attention.

When Vicky came back the week after this regression, she sat down and began to speak lovingly of her step-father. "You know, I really have started looking at him in a different way since I had that experience."

She realized through the regression that the anger she had toward her real father had been wrongfully directed toward her step-father. In retrospect she was sure that he had always "turned the other cheek" toward her resentment. Although she had been mean to him, her step-father had always been kind and attentive to her needs.

Vicky's past-life regression was effectively used as a way to pry into her home life. What might have taken several sessions to uncover in traditional therapy was reached in one hypnotic regression. The result for Vicky was a more acceptable way of regarding her step-father.

Trait #9: Regressions May Affect Medical Conditions

In rare instances, subjects may report dramatic improvement— even spontaneous resolution—of physical symptoms following a past-life regression. There is a chapter in this book devoted to this phenomenon. But one case study that I'll discuss here is a woman I'll call Anne. She had frequent and severe headaches. Although she had no organic problems, like a tumor, and she had long ago stopped drinking anything with caffeine, she was unable to control this insidious problem without a large daily dose of aspirin.

She came to me for a hypnotic regression, "just to see what is there." I took her into a hypnotic trance and found her experiencing very bad times in ancient Egypt. Here is what she had to say after the regression.

I was living in an Egyptian city that was being attacked by invaders from another country. In the hypnotic trance I could see them descending upon the city, ready to rape and pillage.

We were all terrified. I could see people running all around me as the attacking soldiers chased us, slashing and stabbing with their weapons.

I could see myself. I was a young woman dressed in white clothing. I was trying very hard to get away, but there was little reason to try, since the soldiers were everywhere.

Suddenly I was caught by several of the invaders. One of them held my arms and one of the others hit me on the head with a club. The pain was incredible. They hit me several times and then dropped me. I could feel my brain swelling as I slowly died.

The pain she described was apparently overwhelming. As she lay on the couch with her eyes closed, hurt was evident in her face and voice.

Discussing this terrible death proved to be a cathartic experience for Anne. She experienced a great deal of emotional release in discussing these feelings and the emotion of the moment. As we talked about her hypnotic regression it became clear that there were many sources of stress and panic in Anne's life. By using this powerful regression experience we were able to pry into many emotions she had previously kept pent up.

Since then we have done several regressions. As a result, the intensity of her headaches has decreased and the amount of headache medication she now takes has been greatly reduced.

The occasional cases of this type are evidence of the powerful connections between mind and body which are being explored by those who study psychosomatic medicine.

Trait #10: Regressions Develop According to Meanings, Not a Historical Timeline

If a subject was regressed to a dozen distinct "past lives" over the course of a year or so, the lives would probably emerge in a series of "lives" which center around an emotional or relationship theme, and not in the chronological sequence in which they would have been lived.

For instance, a subject may have a couple of experiences that deal with his attitudes toward members of the opposite sex, followed by a series of two or three lives which embody various ways of dealing with aggression, followed by a cluster of lives in which issues of dependence on others seem paramount.

The primary feature revealed in the "past lives" of a subject seems not to be that person's role in history, but rather the person's psychological and spiritual development. This is yet another feature of these experiences which makes "past-life therapy" possible.

Trait #11: Past-Life Regressions Become Easier with Repetition

Generally speaking, the more a person tries, the easier it becomes to enter into a past-life experience.

That proficiency seems to come with repetition. The subject also feels more and more "natural" and at home with the regressed state.

There may be temporary setbacks; resistance to the state may reemerge due to present-life stresses or other distracting factors, but overall the subject will experience greater and greater ease in entering the regression state.

Trait #12: Most Past Lives Are Mundane

Although popular belief has it that almost everyone who has regressed to a past life claims to have been Napoleon or Cleopatra, I have found only a few subjects who identify with a known historical figure. Instead, most of the lives that appear are typical lives of the period to which they regress.

It isn't uncommon to have people expecting to find they are someone like Joan of Arc or General Longstreet in their past life. They are usually disappointed to find themselves an ordinary slave or just a foot soldier in the Civil War.

THE PLEASING MIND

Traits are like tire tracks on a dirt road: They might let you know that a vehicle has been there, but they don't necessarily tell you what kind of vehicle it was.

As a result of my research, I knew I was no longer a skeptic, but I didn't know what I was no longer skeptical about. Isolating the traits or "symptoms" of PLRs meant that I knew what to expect from a hypnotically regressed patient. But it didn't mean that what they were perceiving had really happened.

The mind likes to please and for that reason it is highly suggestible. When given the opportunity, it will fill in gaps with great aplomb. And when given the focused leisure time that hypnotism presents, it will often occupy itself with self-made fantasies.

Some of the very first astronaut research illustrates this. Astronauts were blindfolded, wrapped in padding, and floated on rubber membranes above a heated pool to simulate the weightlessness and isolation of outer space. In almost every instance, the total lack of sensation led them to become confused and disoriented. Frequently they experienced wild "dreams" which seemed to spring from nothing other than the brain's need to stimulate itself. Similar research with more earthbound subjects has rendered similar results.

Skepticism aside, past-life regression analysis clearly offers some important new opportunities for the psychotherapist. After conducting almost one hundred hypnotic regressions for my research, it was obvious to me that this method offers a quick and innovative way to find out, at least partially, what is troubling the subject.

In almost every hypnotic regression that I have conducted, the subject's "past-life" memory mirrors a conflict in his or her current life. By hypnotically regressing them, I am able to arrive at the root of the problem quickly. Instead of spending hours of "couch time," the patient is able to fully face his problem early in therapy and spend more time learning to cope with it than finding it.

Believers in reincarnation say that this mirroring occurs because a conflict in a past life must repeat itself life after life until it is resolved. Maybe this is true. Who's to say otherwise? But I do believe that past-life regressions deal with mental conflict in a unique and effective way, one whose value should be realized even by those who don't believe in past lives and reincarnation.

That is why I continued to examine them.

II

—

Uses
of
Past-Life
Therapy

3

The Healing
Power of Past Lives

When I was in medical school it would have been heresy to suggest that the mind could cause or cure a physical illness. In the eyes of the medical establishment, mind and body were as separate as church and state.

These days it is practically heresy to suggest that the mind doesn't have some control over physical illness. For instance, studies at Harvard have shown that the happier the person, the stronger their immune system. Links have been shown between heart disease and attitude, especially the tendency of anger to constrict blood vessels and clot blood. And respiratory problems such as asthma have been deemed to have "emotional triggers," which means they manifest themselves as a response to an emotional event.

Now researchers are even looking for connections between the mind and the onset of cancer.

It should come as no surprise then that regression therapists are also testing the effects of past-life regressions on a variety of diseases.

To find out what these therapists were using their talents on, the late psychotherapist Helen Wambach conducted a survey of 26 past-life therapists with a total of 18,463 patients among them. Her survey revealed that 24 of the 26 therapists did regression work related to physical symptoms. Of these, 18 reported that 63 percent of their patients had improved at least one physical symptom after therapy aimed at a specific illness. Of these patients who improved, 60 percent of them improved after re-experiencing a past-life death and 40 percent improved after reliving other traumatic past-life experiences not related to death.

I have frequently seen past-life therapy used successfully in curing diseases, both physical and mental. Most of the diseases successfully treated by regression therapy are those with "emotional triggers," diseases that react in one way or another to emotional situations. These are diseases such as asthma and some other respiratory problems; many skin diseases such as dermatitis and warts; ulcers, hypertension, headaches, and some gastrointestinal disturbances.

I don't know exactly why past-life regressions work in curing some illnesses. But it reminds me of something Albert Einstein said many years ago: "It is possible that there exist emanations that are still unknown to us. Do you remember how electrical currents and 'unseen waves' were laughed at? The knowledge about man is still in its infancy."

What Einstein said is, of course, true. Each of us has a large, unused portion of the brain. Estimates are that we use only 40 percent. The remaining 60 percent has a mysterious function. As an added mystery, each of our cells contain thousands of genes, yet we know the purpose of only a few of these elements that form everything we know as mankind.

POWERS OF MIND

There are many examples to be drawn from psychiatric literature that show the power mind has over body. But perhaps my favorite illustrations are those people who have experienced the stigmata, the supernatural appearance of wounds on the hands and feet of devout Christians. These wounds appear on the same spots where Christ was nailed to the cross during the crucifixion. In some cases bleeding has even appeared on the side of the individual, the place where the Roman spear gashed Jesus, and around his or her forehead, where the crown of thorns pierced him.

Of those who have experienced the stigmata, perhaps the

most intriguing example is Padre Pio, a Capuchin monk who lived in Foggia, Italy.

In 1918, while saying Mass, Padre Pio fell into a trance and then collapsed. Attending physicians found bleeding wounds on his hands, feet, and side.

At first even the Vatican was skeptical of Padre Pio's claim that the bleeding wounds were "an act of God." But the wounds never healed. They bled constantly, sometimes soaking several tissues a day.

Finally, after years of bleeding (and observation, to make sure the wounds weren't self-inflicted) the Vatican recognized the stigmata wounds of Padre Pio as being divine. Many medical researchers feel that Padre Pio's case is simply one of wish fulfillment that happened as a result of self-hypnosis.

Although some examples of the stigmata can be proven to be fraud, many can only be explained as the end result of religious fervor, a prime example of wishful thinking.

I bring up the stigmata to illustrate the incredible powers of the mind over normal physical functions.

There are other examples of hypnosis having a profound effect upon bodily responses.

For instance, it is known that by deeply hypnotizing some subjects and telling them that a hot object has been placed on their skin, blisters may actually appear as a result of the suggestion.

There is a well-known case in the medical literature in which a child was hypnotized and cured of *icthyosis*, a congenital disease that gives the skin a dark and scaly appearance.

In that case, a physician hypnotized the child and gave him the suggestion that the lesions would disappear. They did so within days.

These examples and others show us that emotions can lead to astounding physical changes.

In the eyes of the medical establishment, the connection between the mind and body becomes more apparent every day. But does this mean that past-life regression therapy is ahead of the times, or does it mean it is simply "far out"?

It's my belief that with some diseases, regression therapy might not be as "far out" as it seems.

ARTHRITIS AS A METAPHOR

In *The Journal of Regression Therapy*, family therapist Dree Miller Dunlap of Camarillo, California tells how regression therapy relieved the pain of arthritis in her shoulders, elbows, wrists, and hands.

Dunlap went through a past-life therapy session to find out specifically why she had arthritis: Here is what she found:

As the regression took place I found myself as a male sixteenth-century Italian physician. I was treating a young girl (about eight years old) who had broken her arm at the elbow. It was necessary to put the bones back in place to set the arm. I violently twisted the child's arm. Bone grated against bone. The child screamed, and I knew that I had deliberately inflicted pain.

I felt confused and humiliated. I didn't like seeing myself as cruel. The confusion arose from the knowledge that I, a good physician who loved children, had acted viciously. This behavior puzzled me. As the regression continued, I learned that I was unhappily married to a woman who did not want children and refused to consider having a family. Anger and bitterness filled our marriage. I inflicted these feelings onto my patients. In my mid-years, my wife died and it was as though a millstone had been removed from my neck. Now I was free to live my life as I pleased. However, I had by this time developed arthritis. My crippled joints made it impossible for me to continue with my practice of medicine. I retired to a small cottage in the country, where I lived quietly, spending most of my time and energy in my garden.

As an old man, I was very close to a young blonde girl who lived nearby. She would come and work with me in the garden. I loved this child dearly. She was about five or six when my time to die arrived. As I lay dying, she brought me a bouquet of flowers and kissed me on the cheek. She seemed to know that I was dying and seemed to accept the naturalness of death. As my spirit rose from my body, I watched her run out the door to fetch someone. As I reviewed and evaluated that lifetime, it was clear that I had misused my healing skills. I had let bitterness and anger dominate much of my life. It was not enough that I had resolved much of that anger later in life—I had not forgiven my wife—I had only been relieved by her death.

A second lifetime emerged, one in which she was a monk in a monastery.

During this same regression, I was led to another lifetime with connections to arthritis. This time I was a monk living a very austere life in a monastery. Again I was working in a garden. I was regularly complaining about the lack of commitment I perceived in my fellow monks. I openly castigated them for not having more respect for God. This theme of criticizing seemed to predominate throughout this life. I reached old age bitter and isolated. The younger monks would laugh at me behind my back. The more I complained, the less they sought to hide their disdain of me. My bitterness deepened even more and I began to complain to God about the inadequacies I saw in others. My last few years of life were spent alone in my cell. My body was racked with pain. The chill dampness of the cell added to my misery. I died alone, in pain, and to the sorrow of no one.

What did these past lives mean in the way of relief from arthritis for Dree? The regressions revealed to her that anger, bitterness, lack of acceptance, unforgivingness, and violation of skill are all factors in her current life. For instance, she recognized her wife in the first regression as being her ex-husband in her current life. It was also this ex-husband who didn't want children after they were married.

"I wish I could say that I was magically changed, instantly

cured, and blissfully happy from that day forward, but that would be missing the main point of what this experience is about." She wrote in her summary,

> My arthritis isn't completely gone. It seems to flare up when I allow anger or impatience or bitterness or unforgivingness into my life. When the pain comes, it serves me as a reminder. If I stop and listen to the message it brings, the pain is soon gone.
>
> Did I really live in sixteenth-century Italy as a physician? Was I really a monk who lived a painful, embittered life in a monastery? I don't know. What I do know is that these stories have substantially contributed to the way I view my life, live my life, and to what I believe about myself and others. . . . I try to walk through this life peacefully, lovingly, seeking to be patient, compassionate, and humble . . . and learning to forgive myself when I don't meet those standards.

It seems to me that there is a strong connection between Dree's emotional state and flare-ups of her arthritis.

SUFFOCATION ASTHMA

In my own practice I have had two patients who were cured of physical ailments through past-life regressions.

In one, a woman in her thirties—we'll call her Mary—had been plagued by asthma since she was a very little girl. This had become such a severe problem for her that it began to interfere with daily functions. She went through standard medical treatment, but the inhaler medicines she was given only served to give her temporary relief.

Out of curiosity—and I daresay as a last resort—she came to past-life therapy.

First we talked about her life. She was happily married to an English professor and by her own assessment had very little stress in her life. She was a homemaker who was happy in the role of managing the household and taking care of their four-year-old daughter.

The asthma attacks came on with very little stress. For instance, the night before our first session, Mary had an attack while fixing dinner! The mere stress of doing something under even the vaguest deadline had triggered an attack.

I made her comfortable on the couch and hypnotized her. She found herself in late-nineteenth-century London, living the life of a housewife in one of those unexceptional row houses that are famous in that city.

She happily recounted the activities in her days: shopping, cooking, caring for the house, sewing. It all seemed quite ordinary.

Then we went forward to the last hour of her life. She saw herself walking through the streets of London on a very foggy day after shopping for a dress. It was a cold day, one that had her bundled up so tightly that the only thing showing was a tiny area of her face so she could see where she was going.

Perhaps she wasn't being very attentive, she said. When she reached her home she fumbled in her purse for the keys, not really paying attention to anything around her. When she opened the door, a man who had been standing behind her on the sidewalk pushed her into the apartment and slammed the door.

She fought to escape, breathing rapidly and thrashing on the couch in front of me as she described the battle. The fight was to no avail. Soon he was on top of her and in a flash her face was covered with a pillow and she was being suffocated.

In the regression she left her body and was able to look down and describe the death scene. When the man finished killing her, he began to ransack the apartment, tearing out drawers and looking through the piles of clothing for cash. When he found none, he kicked her and raced out the door.

In this out-of-body state she began to describe feelings of loss. She was sad to have been deprived of life, especially at such an early age and in such a tragic fashion. She was also heartbroken at missing any future life with her young husband.

That one session gave her relief from her asthma. She feels that this experience truly represented a past life. As she put it after the regression, "What else could it be? And where else could it have come from?" She believes that since it happened in a past life, it shouldn't really affect her current life at all.

Now when she feels an asthma attack coming on, she remembers where it came from. "I remind myself that this man killed me in a previous life, but he really shouldn't have an effect on my current one."

The results for Mary have been far fewer asthma attacks and a great reduction in the amount of medicine she must take.

A HIGH-PRESSURE SITUATION

Anne, the patient I referred to earlier, had been a victim of high blood pressure for several years. She had taken hypertension medicine and watched her diet carefully, but without much success. It seemed that no matter what regimen she followed, her blood pressure would eventually become elevated. She complained about it a lot, but neither of us ever thought there could be a past-life connection.

Then one day she asked me to perform a regression just to "see what was back there." We weren't searching for a connection to her hypertension. If I had to describe what we were doing I would simply call it a recreational regression.

What happened was quite astounding.

As I described previously, Anne found herself in a small city in Egypt. She came into this existence on what was probably the last day of her life. The city was surrounded by hordes of an unnamed aggressor. Most of the army defending this town were dead and now panic was in the air as the invading forces moved in for the kill.

After the session, she described what she saw:

It finally became horrifying. I could see people running all around me through the streets as attacking soldiers chased us, slashing and stabbing with their weapons.

The soldiers were very selective in who they killed first. They would hit the women with their fists to get them out of the way but keep them alive. It was the men they wanted to kill first.

They would stab them several times, pouring their blood all over the streets. Then they would trample over their bodies and search for other men. Soon it was clear that only the women would be left.

I was a young woman in these scenes and I felt a very intense pressure to get away. Yet it was no use. Every way I looked was blocked. I found myself running with other women but there was really no place to run. We just pounded aimlessly through the streets. Everywhere I turned there seemed to be another group of foreign soldiers.

Finally they closed in on the women. One by one we were pulled out of this huddled group by soldiers. I was one of the first to be taken. An angry soldier pulled me toward him and when I resisted he simply drove a knife into my stomach and let me fall.

That is all I remember.

The pressure she described was apparently overwhelming. As she lay on the couch with her eyes closed, fear was evident in her face and voice. She appeared to be extremely frustrated as she described her fruitless attempts to flee from this deadly enemy.

Afterwards we discussed the events of the regression. They had been very realistic, said Anne. She described them as being "more than a dream," and feeling almost as though they had happened only days before.

She experienced a great deal of release in discussing these feelings of panic. It was clear that the release of emotions that occurred in "reliving" this experience was a relief.

In later sessions we talked about the origin of panic in her life using this as a starting point to discuss sources of stress in her present life. Soon, as a result of the catharsis brought about by her past-life regression, Anne began to freely talk about her relationship with her boss, who caused fear and anxiety by never being happy with her work. She also worried secretly about her relationship with her husband. Although there were no specific problems in their marriage, she was still fearful that the closeness they had once experienced was disintegrating.

Since then we have done several regressions followed by therapy sessions. Her blood pressure has come under control and the amount of hypertension medicine she now takes has been greatly reduced.

Generally, when regressions affect some disease, the disease tends to be psychosomatic. Was it possible that Anne's experience was just an unconscious metaphor for her tendency to panic and act stressful with the slightest provocation? Or did these events that seemed to have come out of the blue really happen, sensitizing her to stress in general? I don't know the answers to those questions.

I do know that now, when she feels her life getting out of control, Anne is able to use this experience as a symbol for her rising blood pressure. In some ways it's just another language for her illness. She is able to relate her out-of-control feelings to her past-life regression, reminding herself what it was like to be chased by invaders in Egypt. "All other experiences pale in comparison to the fear I felt when that happened." The past-life regression has served to calm her down by giving her an emotional reference point. No matter what the problem, she knows it can get no worse than the experience in her regression.

POST-NASAL REGRESSION

An intriguing solution to an ordinary medical problem was presented by George Schwimmer in *The Journal of Regression Therapy*. It was mentioned to him by one of his hypnosis students that the root cause of his post-nasal drip might be in a past life. Perhaps, the student suggested, it was caused by "inner crying" over some deep-felt loss in another life.

To test this theory, Schwimmer was regressed by Bill Clema, an instructor in past-life work. Here were the results as told by the patient:

Bill took me to a past life through a series of visualizations, and when I arrived there he asked me what surface I was standing on.

I was totally puzzled by his question. I could see nothing at this time, but I felt that I was standing on some very peculiar surface, which gave when I stepped on it, although it wasn't mud. I suddenly got an impression of a large wooden vat, but I dismissed it. That's ridiculous, I thought. Bill said, "Well, I think you're standing on grapes in a vat." That was exactly what I had seen and had refused to tell him.

I was a barefoot winemaker in a winery, about twenty-three years old, wearing only pants rolled up to my knees, standing in a vat, somewhere in seventeenth-century Spain. I was laughing and joking with others in the room as I crushed the grapes under my moving feet. Bill asked me various questions about my life there, including if I had a girl. "Oh yes," I said softly, "she's very beautiful." I loved her very much and felt her calm, steady love in return. Suddenly the inner screen of my mind went black and I felt only pure terror. Time stood completely still: I was in a total void.

"What's the matter?" Bill asked. I couldn't answer—I didn't want to see or speak or acknowledge what I had flashed on. He asked me again and my throat and tongue refused to function. I finally forced myself to reply, although I still could see nothing on my inner screen.

"She's dying," I said, feeling emotionally dead inside myself.

"What happened?" Bill asked gently.

It was an accident, I told him. A horse that had been drawing a wagon had bolted and run her down. Both horse and wagon had passed over her body and she was dying of internal injuries. At this point my inner vision returned, and I saw myself kneeling by the side of her bed, devastated. Her head was to my left, and her pallet was against a wall in front of me, with a window behind her revealing a bright sky. I felt empty as I watched her labored breathing and felt life slipping out of her body.

"Are you crying?" Bill questioned.

"No," I replied.

"Why not?"

"Men should not cry."

I was feeling tremendous grief, and when Bill told me that it was all right for me to cry, I began to sob. My body became racked with anguish, and I could feel the grief rising as waves of energy surging through my body, flowing up through my torso and out my throat. My entire body shook with spasms and sobs for several minutes. The genie of grief had been freed from the bottle of self-control which I had built around it hundreds of years ago.

Had Schwimmer really experienced a past life? He doesn't know. He does know, however, that the grief was real and the emotional release was therapeutic. His post-nasal drip has almost become a problem of the past.

MIND OVER BODY

The notion of illness being brought on by the mind is a new one. Even the word psychosomatic ("relating to, involving or concerned with bodily symptoms caused by mental or emotional disturbance," according to Webster's Ninth New Collegiate Dictionary) is relatively new to the English language. The very idea that the mind could create pathological conditions in the body was met with derision by the medical profession.

Research has changed such thinking. Now the medical community readily admits that there is a lot about the mind/body relationship that they don't understand. They now recognize a host of fascinating phenomena—some of which can be reproduced in a laboratory and some which can't.

These phenomena are among the most puzzling we doctors have to deal with.

One of these is the stigmata, which we have already discussed. This is an event in which people of a strong religious persuasion will suddenly erupt with similarly placed wounds to those that Christ had on the crucifix. They will start bleeding from their palms and their feet, or from their side or forehead.

How this happens is not really understood. But the fact that it does happen is well-documented in the medical literature.

A recent and profound case of this happened in California in 1974. A young black girl who was not a Catholic started spontaneously bleeding from the hands and feet after reading a very emotional text about the crucifixion of Christ.

What does the stigmata mean? Is the mind able to will or make wounds open up in the body? We don't know for sure, but anecdotal evidence tells us that the mind/body connection is much more complex than we thought.

Another phenomenon that is very puzzling is that of "hex death," the killing of a person by placing a spell on them. It doesn't make sense that a person could basically wish another person to death. Yet once again, there are many cases of this in the medical literature, where people have been placed under a hex, only to die in a short period of time.

One such case published in the medical literature a few years back was that of a middle-aged man who had always been dominated by his mother. She had ruined two of his marriages by constantly voicing her disapproval of his wives. Then he married a third time to a woman she didn't object to and had a successful marriage.

Problems began when he decided to sell his share of the business he had run for many years with his mother and retire with his new wife. That idea didn't sit well with his mother. She promised him that if he sold, "dire consequences would occur." Shortly after that declaration, he became very ill.

Over the next six months he was in and out of the hospital with physical problems for which the doctors could find no organic cause. What they did notice though was that he would go home from the hospital in high spirits and feeling perfectly well, only to return to the hospital after spending time with his mother.

On his last day of life, the patient visited his physician who declared later that he was in good spirits and feeling fine. At about six that evening he spoke to his mother by telephone. By 6:30 he was dead.

In reconstructing the phone call, his physician found that the mother had said, "No matter what the doctors tell you, if you sell this business there will be dire physical consequences." In his case the dire consequences were death.

On a more scientifically reproducible level, we do know that the mind can have subtle effects upon the chemical processes of our body.

A recent study conducted by Dr. Lee Berk of Loma Linda University has actually shown that following mirthful laughter, the immune response of the body is measurably improved.

What do these things mean? I think they are proof of the effect emotions have on our physical—as well as mental—well-being.

In many cases I have found that past-life regressions go quickly to the very heart of emotion. This shouldn't be a great surprise. Nor should it really be a surprise that people improve their physical condition after undergoing successful regression experiences. After all, it is not uncommon for patients in regular psychotherapy to overcome physical illness after extended therapy.

With regressions, the mental problems causing an illness are often tapped much more quickly.

ILLNESS: A REINCARNATIONIST'S VIEW

Regression therapists who believe in reincarnation take a metaphysical view of illness. They believe that we may choose our illnesses as a lesson, much in the same way that we choose to do unpleasant things in this lifetime because they will make us better or healthier individuals.

Here is their viewpoint: We come into this life from another level of reality. We might well know from this other perspective that we survive bodily death. Knowing this, we might decide to have an illness just to know what that experience is like.

Even in this present life, we go through many painful experiences. An example of this is the act of confession in the Catholic church. People may know that this is a painful experience while they are going through it, but they also know they will have a better state of mind when it is over. Surgery is like that too. We submit ourselves to surgery, not because it feels good, but because we know we'll feel better when it's over.

Illness is an altered state of awareness. Each illness involves its own particular alteration in a person's state of consciousness.

I know this to be true from an illness of my own. I was afflicted for many years with severe hypothyroidism. All during this time, the world seemed heavy, cold, thick, and very inert. Even getting through the day was a monumental effort. And yet I didn't fully realize this until I was treated for some time with thyroid tablets. Then very suddenly one day, everything became bright and warm.

It was only after my recovery that I was able to look back and see that my perception of the world was changed by this illness.

Illness can shape our entire perception of reality. Even something as simple as a sore throat changes the way we view the world. Next time you have one, notice that nagging pain looms very large in your environment.

We all seek altered states of awareness, even in this life. Religious ecstasy is one example. People will go to enormous lengths to participate in religious activities that change their state of consciousness. And people who take drugs are usually doing it to alter their state of awareness.

A regression therapist who believes in reincarnation described life this way: It feels like waiting in line to go on a roller coaster ride. They say that when a person is in line to buy a ticket for that ride, something inside them knows that when they are upside down at ninety miles per hour, they aren't going to want to be there. Still they go ahead and buy the ticket anyway because the thrill is unavoidable.

Life is the same way, say reincarnationists. The fact that we are going to have certain illnesses or disasters is secondary to the fact that we are going to learn a lot about ourselves on a spiritual level as we return again and again for the ride of life.

TREATING PHOBIAS: A STUDY

Successful treatment of traditionally physical ailments with past-life regressions puts those illnesses into the realm of a mentally treatable disease, similar to that of a phobia.

Phobias are an exaggerated and usually inexplicable and illogical fear of a particular object or class of objects. Past-life regressions have been successful in treating phobias because they serve to bring these fears to the fore, explaining them on a conscious level.

In a study conducted by Johannes M. Cladder of The Netherlands that dealt with the treatment of difficult phobics (patients who'd had previous psychotherapy and in some cases hospitalization), 20 out of 25 patients got rid of their phobias through past-life regression therapy. It took the patients who had been previously hospitalized an average of fifteen sessions to improve, while the patients who had not been hospitalized showed significant improvement after ten sessions.

Cladder concluded that past-life therapy is a quick and effective means of dealing with phobias.

EXTINGUISHING SABRINA'S FEAR

This example comes to me from a West Coast therapist and deals with a woman's fear of fire.

We'll name this woman Sabrina. She was plagued with such a powerful fear of fire that she couldn't light a match without becoming hysterical. She couldn't sit by a fire and enjoy its warmth, nor could she walk into a restaurant where there were lighted candles without feeling the heat of her phobia. It was even difficult for Sabrina to talk about fire during therapy without becoming extremely upset.

The incident that finally brought Sabrina to past-life therapy was something that happened in a college American history class. In a discussion of early American religion, the professor brought up the subject of the Salem witch trials. This was a period of mass hysteria in America during which several women were tortured and some even burned at the stake for the invented crime of being a witch.

Sabrina began hyperventilating when the subject of witches came up. She tried to gain control of herself but was so shaken that she finally had to leave class.

She came to the regression therapist to see if there was anything in a previous life that might be causing this phobic response.

The therapist hypnotized her, taking her to the last day of her last life:

> I could see myself in frightening clarity. I was a young girl—probably about fourteen—who was being tied to a stake in a place that I know was in France.
>
> There was a crowd around me cheering and yelling. I got the idea that they had done this sort of thing many times before for recreation.
>
> I was horrified. I knew there was no way out of the ropes that I was tied with but still I struggled and fought the bondage.
>
> I was able to tell why I was being burned. I had inadvertently aborted my baby by taking medicine that was given to me by a woman accused of witchcraft. I wasn't being accused of being a witch. But because I had taken this woman's medicine, the judges in this town thought that I was in league with the devil.
>
> I didn't mean to lose this baby. I told them that I had just taken some medicine because I was sick.
>
> They didn't believe me and here I was, about to be burned to death for something I didn't mean to do.
>
> I could see myself in utter terror as they lit up the wood that was stacked around me. I was screaming and choking. I could feel the heat crawl up my legs and start to sizzle my skin.
>
> I didn't die quickly enough. The pain of the fire moved quickly up my body and began to burn my clothing from my body. My hair caught on fire and the smoke was burning my lungs like hot acid.
>
> Only after all that pain did I die.

Although it might not sound like it, Sabrina's past-life regression was a relief. She now felt that she knew why she had been having these terrible fear attacks whenever she found herself in the presence of fire.

The hysterical nightmares that used to plague her have disappeared. Although she doesn't seek out fire, she doesn't hide from it either. Sabrina can now relax in a candlelit restaurant. She has even been known to sit around the campfire with friends.

THE MAN CHILLER

Fear of men is not an uncommon experience. Women are often turned off to the other gender after experiencing abusive relationships or other problems that they don't want to risk coping with in another relationship.

Occasionally, though, a therapist gets a patient like Maria. She was afraid of men, but when asked why, she could offer no good reason. She had simply always been afraid of them. Regular psychotherapy failed to get at the root of her problem, and Maria decided to see a past-life regression therapist.

The therapist found Maria to be physically attractive. She was not gay and in fact found herself drawn to many men. However, she found that she could hardly have a conversation with a man without experiencing serious distress. She had tried dating once or twice, but found that a normal relationship with a man was nearly impossible.

Her basic complaint was that she distrusted men. Even ones who appeared to be nice were not to be trusted, she said. She wanted desperately to overcome this extreme distrust, even to the point of doing something like past-life therapy, which she didn't believe in.

In the course of several sessions, the therapist took her through many lifetimes. In each of them, she had been seriously abused by men. Finally she found herself in her current life, experiencing an interesting revelation. I'll begin with her first experience.

Regression #1: Frontier Justice

I was in the old West in a town where I wasn't particularly popular. I was running a ranch, which most of the people in town considered to be a man's work. On top of that I was a little crustier than I should have been. I was snappy and likely to bite the head off anyone who talked to me.

I remember coming to town one day and noticing that the people on the sidewalks were looking at me and whispering quietly to one another.

I ignored them and kept riding on. Then I noticed that several of the men were saddling up and following me. Then I heard someone say, "She's the one who stole that horse." I knew then that I was being pursued for a crime that I didn't commit.

Instead of stopping and defending myself like I should have, I decided to run. That decision was a mistake, since they then thought I had actually stolen the horse.

They caught me by a river and asked me where I had hidden the horse. Instead of simply telling them that I didn't steal it, I arrogantly called them names and said they were too stupid to find the right person.

That was when it ended for me in this life. They marched me down to the river and held my head underwater until I died.

Regression #2: The Beheading

I was a simple shop girl in a medieval European town. We sold fine clothing and did a very good business with officials who ran the city.

One of these men took a liking to me. He was some kind of middle-level official—he may even have worked for the church. He began to get sexually interested in me. One evening he asked if I would like to go home with him. I told him no but he kept insisting. When I became more forceful, he became more angry. He said I would regret rejecting him and then he left.

Soon I did regret it. I was taken away by soldiers and placed on trial, if that is what it could be called. He accused me of being a witch and I was not allowed to testify in my behalf.

I was convicted of the crime of being a witch and sentenced to be beheaded in the public square. That is the last I remembered of that life.

Regression #3: Tobacco Road

I remember little of this lifetime and I think I'm glad of that. I lived in a shack in the woods with several children and a mean husband.

We were poor white trash. All the children were filthy and they had torn clothing that was clearly handed down from one child to the next.

My husband was an awful person. He called himself a farmer but he really did little of that. He spent most of his time drinking and playing cards with other "farmers."

One day, he just left. It was that simple. He was gone and the rest of us were left to fend for ourselves. I remember the depressing feeling that taking care of eight or nine kids would leave anyone. I knew we were going to be near starvation in no time.

Regression #4: This Lifetime

In her final regression session, Maria found herself not in a past life, but in her own early childhood.

I found myself as a child, not in a past life, but in my own early childhood.

I looked around and realized that I was at my own third birthday party. All around me were my little friends. We had hats on and we were eating ice cream with spoons and behaving like children that age behave.

I noticed that my mother wasn't happy. In fact, she was quite angry at my father. He was drunk and mumbling his displeasure at having all of these tiny children in his house.

Finally my mother blew up! She began yelling at my father, telling him she was tired of him being drunk all the time while she tried to hold the family together.

At first he was shocked and ashamed. But that slowly turned to anger as it became clear that he was being humiliated in front of all of the neighbors. He began to yell at my mother and call her names. Then he rushed for the utensil drawer and pulled out a butcher knife!

He took a couple of swipes at my mother but was grabbed from behind by a couple of neighbors before he could do any physical damage.

I think the party broke up shortly after that happened. I don't remember much more about it, except that I cried for a long time because I was afraid daddy was going to kill my mom.

That experience in Maria's current life was just as buried as her past-life traumas. On the conscious level, she didn't remember it any more than she remembered being drowned by a posse. Yet it was the result of this final regression that really opened things up for Maria. She was able to remember many childhood traumas and face the sad realization that her relationship with her father had been one built on fear, not love.

Although she still has problems in her relationships with men, she is at least able to deal with them on a day-to-day basis.

And, according to the therapist I got this story from, Maria is still discovering her mysterious past through past-life therapy.

FEAR OF FAILURE

Another regression therapist told me the story of Angela, a woman who was unable to complete any task for fear of failure. As soon as she started most projects, she found that she couldn't finish them. Whether it was writing a letter, remodeling her home, applying for a different job, there was almost nothing she could finish.

She lived in constant fear that people would be critical of her. Lately her problems had become even more acute. On the job as an airline stewardess, for instance, Angela was having performance anxiety when merely offering drinks to people after takeoff. Because her problems were beginning to interfere with her work, Angela decided to attempt past-life therapy.

Angela is a petite blonde with the type of attitude that could best be described as "perky." Her current life contrasted sharply with the one that came up in her regression. As soon as she went under, Angela found herself as a fierce gladiator.

Here is how she described her regression:

I immediately felt very masculine and strong. I looked down at myself and could see that I was dressed in heavy protective armor. I was holding a sword, practicing different thrusts and swipes with this weapon as a coach told me what to do to improve my technique.

I was in a dirt arena, practicing to kill people. I was a gladiator in Rome.

It was obvious from the way I was treated that I was a very special gladiator. For instance, the other less important warriors were all being coached in groups. I had my own coach. Also, in another scene, I was taken to a special dining table to eat, one that was far away from the ordinary gladiators and that had better food.

In a later scene I could see myself being driven through the streets of a city. People were lining the sides of the road just to get a glimpse of me. I could tell that I was a major sports hero and that it meant a lot for them just to be able to see me. I felt very proud of this fact.

I was then taken to the last day of this life. I could see myself from a third-person perspective, as if I were watching television. I was lying in a dirt arena that was surrounded by a yelling, screaming crowd. I had a gaping wound in my side that was bleeding badly. Standing over me was the gladiator who had finally gotten the best of me. He had his sword held high and was asking the crowd if I should live or die!

The most horrible realization for me was that they wanted me to be killed! I realized then that I was only loved for the entertainment I could bring the public. My life really meant nothing to them. They had turned on me and now they were cheering my death as though I was a lowly and unimportant gladiator!

In discussing her regression, Angela said that she perceived this moment as one of total and complete humiliation. She said that as he/she was dying there in that arena, she vowed never to put herself in a public situation in which he/she could be humiliated again.

Angela thought for certain that it was this past life as a gladiator that made her fear the public. Whenever she faced the public or even thought about it, this deep-seated fear in humiliation resurfaced and she withdrew into herself.

The therapist who treated Angela said that she had one of the quickest turnarounds she had ever witnessed. After only five sessions of therapy, she became a new person, virtually fearless in public. She initiated new programs at the airline and even accepted an offer to do a television yoga show. No longer did she feel as though something was holding her back. For her, the world started opening up.

The fascinating thing to me about this case was that Angela's problems with fear of failure were in this life, yet traditional therapy would never have found out that her problems were rooted in a past life (or at least something perceived as such). For her, regression therapy was like sending a drill bit down into the unconscious to find what was down there. Without this therapy, she would have wrestled with this problem for years to come and maybe never have come to grips with it.

SYMBOLS FOR SYMBOLS

How can it be that phobias seem to be alleviated by these little stories? I believe it's because phobias themselves are symbolic illnesses. Usually the object a person is phobic about is just representative of a neurotic condition. The phobic object itself is not to be taken literally.

From that perspective, it isn't surprising that these stories come out of what is essentially a symbolic condition. The stories about conflicts and relationships and so on that we hear of in the past-life regression might simply be a rearrangement of these symbolic problems, giving individuals new insight into their psychological conflicts.

So if someone is afraid to go out into public—*agoraphobia*, it is called—then Freudian therapists might feel that their real fear is one of unbridled sexual activity. Or a fear of heights goes back to a lack of basic trust between, say, a mother and son.

Past-life regressions allow these symbols to express themselves in a theatrical form. In a way it is role-playing of the mind, an effective means of coping with those larger-scale problems.

DEPRESSION'S MAGIC BULLET

Perhaps the most effective use of past-life therapy comes when it is used against depression. No one knows for sure why this is true; however, I am willing to make an educated guess based upon research done in the field of near-death experiences.

Near-death experiences (NDEs) are spiritual events that occur in many people who almost die. A person having a heart attack, for instance, may view resuscitation efforts on himself from a vantage point outside his own body. He may then have the sensation of being sucked up a tunnel that leads to a heavenly landscape with brightly lighted people. An NDEer may see a Being of Light (often described as God or Allah) who takes him on a life review.

At first it was assumed that reading about near-death experiences or having one would increase the likelihood that a depressed person—someone who had attempted suicide, for instance—would become more depressed. The reasoning was that evidence of life after death would push a person to end this life so they could begin another and possibly better one.

To test this theory, a researcher had a group of people who had attempted suicide read accounts of NDEs while another group of equal size was treated in the usual fashion. Rather than increasing the suicide rate, learning about NDEs *decreased* it.

Why? The researchers found that learning about a life after life increased the level of hope in a person. Rather than wishing for his or her life to end, the patient felt hope, and not despair, by evidence of another life.

I think successful past-life regression therapy has much the same effect upon a seriously depressed person as do near-death experiences.

I find that depressed patients who have undergone past-life therapy are then much more positive and optimistic about life. As one patient put it: "The thought that I may have lived before and will probably live again means that I can ease up a little in this life, that maybe I can stop taking things so seriously."

Many depressed patients find some of the sources of their depression in a past life. The explanations for why this happens vary, depending upon the therapist's school of thought.

Some feel that there really is no such thing as a past life to begin with. What the patient is really seeing in his regression are experiences from the present life, fabricated around the problem.

So, for instance, a person who is depressed about a divorce may take that failed relationship and combine it with images from books read as a child and come away with a "past-life regression" in which the wife is a slave girl who is dominated by the plantation owner.

A regression therapist who believes in past lives might say that the marriage ended in divorce because the relationship had been a bad one in a previous life. The therapist would probably say that this bad relationship would repeat itself life after life until the couple finally got it right.

And so on, not just for divorces but for other mental problems and sources of depression as well. Which explanation is true? That question really can't be answered. But the answer isn't as important as are the results.

BATTLING DEPRESSION, REINCARNATION STYLE

Atlanta past-life therapist Diane Seaman, a believer in reincarnation, thinks that problems like depression can be handed down to a person's next life through "cellular memory." It isn't until these problems are dealt with openly that they leave a person's psychological makeup in this life and in subsequent ones.

As an example, Seaman points to a patient who had tried

several months of traditional psychotherapy to overcome his severe depression. While in this course of traditional therapy, he
began to have a sense that he had lived before. Very vivid dreams
had him involved in trench warfare in World War I.

Although he didn't believe in past-life therapy or in reincarnation, he was interested in the origin of these dreams and in
finding out why they were happening. A friend referred him to
Seaman and he reluctantly agreed to try hypnotic regressions.

Although he was quite vocal in his disbelief in reincarnation,
Seaman found that he was desperate and willing to try almost
anything to discover the source of his depression. As she put
it, "He was ripe for treatment. If someone comes to you in
extreme discomfort they are then ready to work through their
problems."

In the regression, the patient found himself deep in the
combat action of World War I. He was a foot soldier at the front,
pinned down most of the time by heavy artillery and machine-gun
fire.

This experience left him steeped in depression over the existence of war and the constant fear of personal extinction.

As he described the fear he was experiencing, Seaman said
that he was breathing heavily and sweating profusely. Fear con-
torted his face as did pain and anguish as he described those
around him being killed.

> It was horrible. There was no way to turn that didn't
> show death. Even when we were down in trenches, the
> artillery shells would fall from the sky and come straight
> down on our heads.

"He had one of the most emotionally charged sessions I have
ever seen," said Seaman, describing it to me later. "In my experience as a therapist I would have to say that there is no way a
person could make up this kind of emotion. The feeling and the
details were authentic and his emotions were simply draining."

Diane Seaman feels that her patient had never dealt with the
trauma of World War I when he was in it. Now, in this life, she

was helping him discharge the pent-up grief that had built up over lifetimes.

Do I agree with this? I don't know. There is certainly little if any scientific proof of reincarnation. But does that mean it doesn't happen? It certainly does not. After all, it was scientists who denied near-death experiences for so many years until proof of them finally became so overwhelming that their existence could not be denied.

But speaking as a psychotherapist, I would have to say that it doesn't matter if these experiences in past-life regressions represent real past lives or not. What matters is that they are becoming recognized as effective tools in psychotherapy.

4

When Past Lives Meet the Present

I rarely encounter a past-life experience that doesn't in some way relate to a problem in the patient's current life.

I think most regression therapists agree with that finding. The real division between regression therapists and their more traditional colleagues begins with the regression therapists who believe in reincarnation and think that we are born together again and again until we solve our problems.

For example, a couple I know were having problems in their marriage. The wife said that the husband was sexually abusive and domineering. The more she pointed out this abusiveness to him, the worse he became. His constant need for sex, she said, was driving them apart.

His story was quite different. She used to like the frequent encounters, he said. For years it was almost "sex on demand," with her as a willing participant. Recently things had changed. She had become moody and resistant, refusing any type of advance.

Regular therapy had failed and now they wanted to attempt past-life therapy to see if they could get at the root of their problem.

The therapist regressed them together. The result was a tale of true love gone awry. Both found themselves together in a previous life. She was a servant girl in a castle in medieval Ireland and he was a knight.

With her it was love at first sight. She gave herself freely and frequently to the knight. With him it was an affair of a different color. He was interested in her only for the pleasure she could bring. He would string her along until he was finished with her. Then he planned to hand her off to one of his fellow knights.

She realized this in a horrible event.

> One night I stole into his chamber after a day of anxiously waiting for the moment. But instead of finding him, I was faced with one of his friends. I tried to leave, but he grabbed me and began pulling my clothing off. I fought him, but my strength was nothing compared to his.
>
> "Don't be upset," he said. "Your knight told me what you've been doing. I can be as much fun as him."

What was the regression therapist's interpretation of this jolting session? It was her opinion that they had been born once more together in order to be able to work out this problem in a new life.

The regression therapist said that they needed to discuss the results of this regression frequently, approaching sex in their "new life" with tender loving care so they wouldn't repeat the offenses of the past life.

This approach worked. However, I had the opportunity to talk to this couple at a later date and came away with a very different conclusion than the therapist.

I questioned the couple about their current lives during the time of their travails. The wife admitted that they had always had an active and rather uninhibited sex life. She also enjoyed it, she said.

But a problem that neither of them had been able to discuss with the therapist was the husband's desire to "swap partners" with another couple. When the wife was told of this desire by her husband, she was devastated. The relationship immediately changed, with the wife no longer interested in sex or closeness in any form and the husband angry that his wife's pleasures had been withdrawn.

They had been unable to discuss the real problem with anyone until now. Why? Because the results of the regression had opened them up. Did they believe they had lived a past life in medieval Ireland? Neither of them was sure. It was possible, they said. After all, the regression experience felt vivid enough to be a memory of real life. More important, however, it had given them a place to start in discussing their current problems.

THE LANGUAGE OF THE UNCONSCIOUS

Are these regressions really memories of past lives? I don't know. Later in this book I will offer several possible explanations for the existence of so-called past lives. But as a medical doctor who has dealt with the mysteries of the mind, I must say that I can neither refute nor support regressions as proof of reincarnation.

Some psychologists and psychiatrists believe that the mind is creating dramas to help it cope with different situations. I like to call this the language of the unconscious. It is a language in which problems are dealt with metaphorically rather than directly. To create these metaphors, the mind draws upon all of its available resources—memories thought to be long gone, images from books and television, pieces of conversation, even events daydreamed and "forgotten" a long time ago.

When it needs to face dilemmas, the unconscious mind creates drama from the material at hand. Under hypnosis, these become memories as real as yesterday's lunch date.

For instance, victims of child abuse frequently forget their experiences on the conscious level until they become sexually active adults. Then, the pain of these childhood traumas bubbles to the surface, affecting their sexual performance but never actually emerging from the subconscious. It isn't until some kind of therapy roots out these problems that they are remembered.

AN IMMIGRANT'S EXPERIENCE

I discovered one such case during the regression of a woman I'll call Linda. When taken back to a previous life, she found herself in a strict Italian family in turn-of-the-century New York City. Her mother was so repressed and fearful of the father that she had the presence of a servant in Linda's regression. She cooked and did the housework but took virtually no hand in raising the children.

The father was a horrible tyrant. He worked as a laborer and would come home exhausted and mean almost every night. He favored his sons and let them run wild. He despised Linda, whom he thought of as being somewhat of a tramp because of her desire to work as a secretary instead of a housewife.

In her regression she is walking home one night after work when she has the horrible realization that she is being followed by a group of men. As she described this event under hypnosis, she grimaced with terror.

I suddenly realized that the men who had passed me a block back were now following me. I speeded up and so did they. Soon, I was running down the street. The streets were dark and I thought I could lose them by ducking into an even darker alleyway. I was wrong.

They followed me into the alley and raped me. One by one all five of them did it. Then they just left me there, crying and beaten.

I got myself together the best I could and went home. As soon as I went into the house it was obvious that something had happened to me. My hair was a mess, my face was bruised and slapped red, and I was crying.

I sat in a chair and pulled my torn clothing together to hide myself. While I cried, my mother left the room and pretended to be working in the kitchen. She didn't say one word the entire time I sat there. She just stayed in the kitchen.

My father did all the talking. He said I deserved it since I insisted on working outside the home like a "common whore." He said he wouldn't even file charges against the men who had raped me because as far as he was concerned, they had done the right thing.

Because of the horror of this regression, I became interested in what connection, if any, there was to her present life. I began a typical therapy session in which I asked her detailed questions about her family life and childhood. I started with the usual biographical questions about date and place of birth and then began to focus intensely on her relationship with her mother and father.

I soon found plenty of connections between her past-life regression and her current life.

Both of her grandparents had emigrated from Italy to New York in the very early part of the century. Her grandfather was a domineering "old world" man. He liked to brag that the women in his family were always women and the men always manly.

As we probed deeper, a sad, dark truth emerged. Linda had been sexually abused by her father. All through her childhood, her father would fondle her and commit various sexual acts with her. She had been frightened by these acts and frequently pleaded with him not to perform them. He ignored her, insisting he had the right to do all of these things. And her mother never once tried to stop her husband from these molestations, although she knew what he was doing.

Was Linda's regression a combination of the above factors—the language of the unconscious—or was her life really repeating itself until it got itself right? I don't know.

I do know, however, that this regression experience helped Linda uncover childhood events that she needed to expose before she could live a normal life.

Let me offer a few more case studies that show how past-life regressions can be a metaphor for problems in one's present life.

LESLIE'S FIERY EXISTENCE

Leslie was going through a period of great difficulties in her life. She was in the middle of a messy divorce from her husband who was fighting viciously with her over their property settlement. On top of that, she was arguing constantly with her adolescent children who didn't want their parents to separate.

As a result of these travails, she had a constant look of anger and sorrow on her face that was rarely broken by smiles.

She came to me to see if past-life regression therapy could help her better understand the problems in her life. The result of her regression was a deep dip into what seemed to be man's earliest beginnings.

> I found myself at the very dawn of civilization, in the midst of a great forest. I was smack in the middle of a group of dancing, chanting people. It was night and the object of this dancing and chanting was a huge fire. It suddenly became clear to me that we were worshiping this fire.
>
> I could feel the heat of the flames and the sweat through my clothes as we danced crazily. I realized after a while that we were dancing to the beat of the flames and not in a random fashion.
>
> The light of the fire was so haunting to us that there seemed to be little else left to live for. We eat and gather food, but we are silent most of the time. It isn't until the fire ritual starts that any of us really feels alive.
>
> At the end of my life, an awful image came to mind. I was able to see it from the air, above where we lived. Our tribe was trapped in a natural geographic bowl by another tribe above us. We had been fighting with these people for a long time and they had finally caught us in this hidden valley where we lived. Rather than fight us with sticks and stones, they chose to burn the forest around us! They started a fire that swept down the bowl and caught our entire tribe in a horrible inferno. In my last scene, I could see this fire rushing toward me and feel the heat and fear. Then that life was over.

Afterwards, Leslie and I discussed the results of her vivid and surprising regression. We determined that, psychologically speaking, the fire represented three things. The first and most obvious was the anger she felt toward her husband and children. She felt this uncomfortable heat from the people she was drawn toward.

It also represented abandonment. Leslie felt she had been deserted by the people she had always cared for. All of her married life, Leslie said that she had been the organizer and caregiver, listening to her husband's complaints about his job, organizing scout troop activities for her children, doing all those things that had earned her the label of "super wife." She had never been the kind of person who just enjoyed life and did things for herself.

Now that she needed help from her loved ones the most, she found that they weren't willing to give of themselves. Instead they were making her life miserable by insisting she stay in the role she had always occupied.

Finally, we determined that the fire represented spiritual quest. Since it had become clear to her that she could no longer fill the role of super mom, she was on a spiritual quest to find out what role she should now fulfill.

Had she really lived this primordial life? Once again, I don't know. The regression experience was a vivid one for Leslie. She was sure she had really danced around such a fire at some point in her existence. Since our regression she has had others and has been able to duplicate the experience in even greater detail.

But, in my opinion, the real strength in this regression was its cathartic effect upon Leslie. The experience gave her a metaphor to hang all of her problems on. It enabled her to speak more freely about the problems that were plaguing her life in the here and now.

KERRY'S FREEDOM

Kerry is so close to her mother that the two of them are practically fused. She is in her mid-thirties, lives at home, and has never been married.

Kerry's life is fraught with responsibility. She is an insurance adjuster by day, a job that she says is very demanding. Four nights a week she attends law school. Any remaining "extra" time is eaten up by study and "family duties."

Those family duties are especially taxing for Kerry. She would like to have a little more time to herself so she can "live a normal existence," which for her would be going out with friends and dating men. However, her mother practically demands that she not do anything without her. "Every time I try to do anything outside the family structure, my mother makes me feel guilty," says Kerry.

Kerry likes being a responsible person who is attentive to her mother's needs. But she would like to live her own life. Kerry readily admits that she is ready for some fun and new experiences. As she puts it, "Life is short, and my mother is making it shorter by not allowing me a longer leash."

Her regression put her into one of the most free lives I can imagine, that of a sailor. Notice how she longs for freedom in this regression and also how she feels about her family.

At the end, I'll tell you an interesting sidelight I discovered as a result of this regression.

Here's Kerry's regression:

I was a man, a sailor, who was looking out at the deep turquoise-blue sea as we came into a port. I could tell that I had no interest in the cargo, only interest in being at sea. Where everyone else was obviously glad to be headed for shore, I was looking forward to my next journey and further adventures.

When I went ashore I was able to change perspective and see myself. I was a small muscular man with tight curly hair and a very serious look on my face. I was walking up a hill into a lower-class neighborhood.

As I walked up this hill, I was able to monitor exactly what I was thinking in this life. I was thinking about my father and how he was always out to sea just as I am now. I remembered him with great fondness and felt a deep emptiness inside at the thought that I would never see him again.

As I was walking up the hill toward my home, there was a lot of vigorous activity going on around me. People were shouting and selling and telling stories in loud and passionate ways. I didn't participate in this joviality. I just walked grimly to my home.

My wife and children were there but I wasn't particularly glad to see them. I was struck by my impersonal attitude toward my children. I greeted them but I didn't kiss or hug any of them. I also had not brought any of them gifts, even though I had been at sea for several weeks and had visited many ports. It was clear that my real attachment in life was the sea.

So for me, home was just a place to stay when the ship was in port. I had sex there and some companionship but for the most part I didn't enjoy my wife or offspring. Where I really came alive was when I was with my mates on the ship. There, I was a cheerful, vibrant person. At home I was impersonal.

I saw this as a defense against attachment. Like my father before me, I wanted to roam the world.

In the next scene, I found myself immediately back in the hold of this ship. Although this was only a cargo ship, it was beautifully appointed. There were carvings and paintings all over the bulkheads and the ship was very clean and well taken care of. These people obviously loved their ships.

I was unable to experience any travel in the regression. All I had was a memory of these trips at sea being the freest feelings one could have. But for the life of me I couldn't remember any specific experiences in other countries.

I could see myself late in life. I was sitting in a chair telling sea stories. I'd had some kind of injury because my legs were badly crippled and prevented me from doing much more than sitting around. I don't know what had happened. My guess is that I fell down into one of the ship's holds or that cargo fell on me.

All I know is that the rest of my life consisted of telling sea stories.

As we already know, Kerry is uncomfortably close to her mother. After this regression she admitted to a growing resentment toward her mother, one that left her almost unable to talk to her at times.

Just like the sailor in the regression, Kerry wasn't glad to see her family anymore. She was at best neutral toward them and at worst, hostile. On the other hand, she is a less repressed person around her friends and colleagues than she is around her mother. When I asked her what the sea might mean to her in this life she said it probably represented freedom from the chains of an over-possessive mother.

I was curious to know why she identified with a male in this regression. When I began to question her about that, she revealed some new information that became very helpful in dealing with her feelings of hostility and repression.

Her father had left the family when she was very young. As best as she could remember, he had offered very little to the family in the way of affection. He didn't appear to care much for her mother or his three young children. He seemed to have used the house as a place to eat and hang his hat, but that was all. Other than that, his presence was hardly known to the family.

Out of need for affection and identity, Kerry became very close to her mother. Ultimately she became dependent upon her.

Kerry thought her father's leaving had had no impact on her. But now she realized that on a subconscious level, she identified strongly with him. In her desire to break from her mother, Kerry believed she had unconsciously become her father.

This realization helped Kerry in long-term therapy. She saw her regression in metaphorical terms—the language of the unconscious. Although she doesn't believe she really lived in a previous life, she does believe that the facts in her life were recombined into a coherent tale. Through this metaphor, she understood her feelings of fusion with her mother.

DONNA, THE DUELING EGOTIST

At the age of sixty, Donna feels a strong need to make a break from her children. She wants them out of the house so she can live the life of a "free woman."

However, she is unable to muster up the courage to simply tell the children to leave. This leaves her feeling inadequate in dealing with her own needs.

To make up for these feelings of inadequacy, Donna has become extremely arrogant with her co-workers. She finds that she argues about nearly everything, as though her ego is on the line at every turn. Her friends have become less friendly as a result of this arrogance, and that worries her.

She came to me hoping that a past-life regression would shed some light on the reason for her runaway ego.

Here is what Donna discovered.

I found myself in Holland or Germany in roughly the fifteenth century. I was a boy who got everything I wanted from my aristocratic family.

The first thing I saw is myself in a cradle, dressed in a fancy white gown. I could see that from even that early age, my parents were trying to control me. They were standing over the cradle trying to convince me not to cry.

Then I move forward rapid-fire through my life. I visited my school and could see that I went to the best schools.

At about sixteen or seventeen, things in the regression slowed down. I could see that my father had died. Although my mother was very shaken by this event, I didn't have any particular reaction to it at all. I was just like him in that I only cared about myself. My mother became very quiet and distressed by my reaction. Once again, she tried to exercise control over me by getting me to become a quiet and more caring individual.

It's too late at this point. I was already just like my father and I didn't give a hoot about changing for any reason.

The rest of this life had me demonstrating the attitude of a very hard-driving merchant. The only time I care what other people think is when they are looking at the goods I have to sell. Then I care a lot.

I can tell that I have no wife or children in this regression. My only friend is my bank account.

I could see another scene vividly. There was a dispute about a horse-drawn coach that I had sold to a man. While I was having dinner with a group of business associates, he charged in and accused me of selling him a bad coach. These days we would call it a lemon.

Since I have been challenged in front of my peers, I challenge this man to a duel.

On one level I needed to fight him since he had insulted my ego. But on another level I was very frightened, since I could see that it really didn't matter to anything in my life if he thought I was a crook or not. I was being totally driven by my ego.

In the final scene, we were in an open space with our guns. We stood back to back and then walked several paces away from each other. Then we spun around and fired.

I remember very vividly seeing a puff of smoke out of this other man's gun and then being hit in the chest by a blinding flash of pain. I seemed to go very quickly. I remember seeing all the spectators gather around me, not really knowing what to do. Then I closed my eyes and faded away.

My thoughts at this point were quite interesting. Although I was losing touch with the world around me, some final thoughts came through loud and clear: **It doesn't matter how you die. Everybody has to die. What matters is that you not become so fixated on honor. This code of honor is entirely artificial and has nothing to do with the soul.**

I find it interesting that her regression dealt very pointedly with the issues of arrogance and ego. The experience was a vivid one for Donna. Although she wasn't sure that it really represented an event from a past life, she was sure that it was a message from her subconscious about the problems of ego that were plaguing her.

What good did this regression do for Donna? It let her know that there are few "all or nothing" situations. It also helped her deal with problems in a less confrontational manner.

TED'S FEARED IDOL

Ted comes from a large family in which the grandmother plays a dominant role. Before his regression, Ted said that a stable relationship existed between all the members of the family. The parents were pleased to have the grandmother living with them, the children all got along with the older members of the family, and so on.

But Ted's regression left the opposite impression. There are symbolic elements in this experience that have him examining his life from a different perspective.

When the regression was over, we talked about the results. Ted's impressions of his family life changed considerably afterwards.

I found myself in a mountain civilization. There was a temple with an idol high in the hills that looked down on the village where we lived. The idol was the center of our universe. None of us knew what resided beyond the village because we could never travel out of the idol's sight. It was the center of some kind of unknown power. From the fear that we all had, my guess is that it held our lives in its hands.

My thought as I looked up at this was: "Will it destroy or harm me?" I could tell that fear was a part of the fabric of this society. Things are kept in the order they are because of that fear.

As I looked around I could see that the houses were made of a flat stone construction and very well put together. Each of them seemed to have the same furnishings, a few clay pots for food, and rough and primitive fabrics.

I felt very little identification with my parents. I didn't have hostile feelings toward them. Instead, the primary closeness I had was with the tribe. There was a great deal of interaction among the people. There weren't lines drawn in their society like there are in ours.

My skin was very dark and my clothing was nothing but panels that covered my genitals.

There were people farming in the valley below. They would till the earth with primitive hoes and rakes, chopping the ground in rows and then planting it with seeds.

It seemed as though everything in this society was

saturated with fear. All of the people did whatever they did out of fear of what was up that mountain.

I found this amazing, because the idol never did anything that I can remember to inspire that kind of fear and reverence. All it did was sit there, which makes sense since it was made of stone. But everyone gave it all of their power. If something went wrong it was because the idol had been offended. If something went right, it was because the idol was happy. It never did anything that I could see, yet all we had and everything that happened to us both good and bad was attributed to this grumpy-faced piece of stone that had been carved by our grandfathers.

I moved forward to about the age of thirty and found myself married to a lovely woman. We had children and I loved them because they made sense out of my life. They got me away from the fear. I don't have many images from that period. I only remember standing in the sun with my family and feeling spiritual warmth for them.

Finally I moved forward to the last moments of my life. I was walking along a cliff with some kind of pack animal and the animal slipped off and fell. I tried to get my hand loose from the cord that was wrapped around its neck but I couldn't. I was pulled over the cliff with it and I died.

This regression changed what Ted had to say about his family.

The idol, he said, reminded him of his grandmother. Although she was quiet most of the time, she ruled the family as a sort of rumbling matriarch.

She always had an opinion to offer, whether it was welcomed or not. She wasn't loud about these opinions, Ted said, but she was so persistent in stating them that they were inescapable. If he didn't listen to her feelings or opinions in the morning, she would repeat them every time she saw him until he finally acknowledged what she had to say.

In therapy, Ted revealed that the family was too close for his comfort and that he hadn't been able to develop as an individual.

The regression was a perfect metaphor for his family, he said, because he could never get out of sight of his family. If his brothers and sisters weren't imposing themselves upon him, then his parents or grandmother were trying to run his life. There was control every way he turned.

In Ted's case, his regression served as a means of expressing his true feelings about his family. It cut through hours of therapy and helped him gain the freedom of expression he wanted in his life.

VICTOR'S MARVELOUS INSTRUMENT

Victor's parents were divorced when he was very young. He has only seen his father twice since he was twelve, but he describes him as a man who is experiencing a perpetual midlife crisis. He is only concerned about his own life and has no real interest in anything in Vic's life. Vic points out that his father didn't even have the decency to help him through school. His mother isn't much better. She is a very depressed and emotional person who shows little interest in her only son. Instead she leaves him feeling guilty whenever he goes to her for any emotional comfort.

When I put him under, he found himself in a large city. The first thing he said was a surprised and questioning, "Where is this place?" Later, he felt it must have been Arabia because the climate was warm and the dress being worn by the people around him consisted of white flowing robes and the sort of turbans one would see in Middle-Eastern desert climes.

I was a scholar. I was about twenty years old. My parents have provided the very best schooling money can buy. They are wealthy and they have great respect for education. They have pushed me to become well-educated and I have gladly accepted the role chosen for me.

I could see my prized possession. It was bright metal and shaped like a sundial that you hold in your hand. It was about two feet in diameter and heavily bejeweled. I got this instrument from a professor. It was an amazing piece of scientific work because it was able to set dates for religious festivals by lining up coordination points with the sun and stars.

I was puzzled by the people I study with at this institution. To them, all studies should be directed toward religion. But I didn't agree with that. I was studying logic and science and I thought that most of the academic work in this university should be directed toward hard sciences.

I was able to flash back in this lifetime and see what my early childhood was like. We lived in a place that was so spectacular it could be described as palatial. There were massive lawns with well-kept gardens. I could see my brothers and sisters and I running around these gardens, playing tag with one another the way children always do.

I moved forward from this scene to a point where I was somewhere in my early twenties. This was an important time in my life. I was hearing voices and had the idea that the prophet Mohammed was speaking to me.

I decided to go on a trek to find out what lay beyond the city. I found myself far from home in a mountain region. It was lush green and beautiful here yet very foreign to a person like me who was from the Arabian deserts. It was in these jungle mountains that I died.

My death happened on a lonely road. I rounded a corner and met a band of men in leather outfits. This clothing covered them all over like some kind of protective wear. They were whiter than me and from their rough and demanding bearing, I would guess that they were soldiers.

They pushed me around and broke into my possessions, rummaging through all of the packs that I had on my pack animal. In one of these packs they found my sacred instrument. They liked it and began looking at it, tossing it back and forth. When they saw the look of terror on my face they began tossing it higher and higher in the air. One of them finally took the instrument and smashed it on the ground. Then they became very rowdy with me because I began yelling at them about the loss I would have because they had destroyed my instrument.

That was when one of them smashed me in the head with a weapon. It was a wooden club shaped like a baseball bat with a fist on the end of it. He hit me once and I went down. I looked up from the ground and saw him raise the club again. I died there on that mountain road.

Vic was puzzled by the images. Arabia? Wealthy parents? A "magic" instrument? Talking to a prophet? On the surface, none of it made sense to him. Then we talked about his present life.

It became obvious that Vic felt directionless without a father as a role model. Vic and I came to the conclusion that the scientific and religious instrument of his regression symbolized the direction, a "fatherly compass," that he never had.

If Vic had not been in a regression state, I would diagnose the hearing of the prophet Mohammed's voice as a case of paranoid schizophrenia. Hearing voices that can't be understood is usually a sign of such a problem.

However, since Vic was in a hypnotically regressed state, his hearing of the voice of the prophet Mohammed probably symbolized the need to hear clearly from his father.

On the whole, I felt that Vic's past-life experience symbolized his deep desire for spiritual guidance.

My recommendation to him was to begin a spiritual quest that would include a great deal of reading and "trying on" a variety of churches.

THE NUMB PRIEST

David is an ex-Marine with no particular religious background. In describing himself, he says he is a sort of wishy-washy Protestant who comes from an unemotional family in North Carolina. "The only way you could get my parents to show emotion would be to break a leg," he said, only half joking. "Then they would just drive fast to the hospital."

He spent four years in the Marines and then left to work in

the real estate business in Atlanta. He admits to being upset by his family's lack of emotion, love, and spiritual guidance. These factors came up throughout his regression.

I saw a very graceful boat in the water. It is made of wood and is long and wide, with pointed ends.

In it was a man with a very bright headdress and a long white robe. This man was a holy man of some sort and I can tell from my feelings as I look at him that he is me.

I was surrounded by four men who are rowing. We are moving through a very clear stretch of water that appears to be a lagoon. As I looked around, I could see hundreds of people standing on the shore watching us as we plied through the water.

I withdrew my hands from inside my robes and cast a handful of leaves and wood chips on the water. This act must have had some religious significance because it drove the people wild.

In the back of the boat was a man who was curled up in a defensive posture, frightened as though someone was going to beat him up.

His hands and feet were bound so tightly that I could see the whiteness of them from the binding. I felt no pity for this man because as far as I was concerned, this was just the rules, the way the religious ceremony was supposed to be conducted.

I walked to the back of the boat and picked this man up by the shoulders and threw him into the water. The crowd on the shore went wild. The man was thrashing about in the water for a few seconds and then the water around him began to roil from the activity of tiny fish that were eating him! The excitement on the shore had almost reached the point of delirium. But I felt nothing, as though I was in some sort of a daze.

At this point I had a flashback to my childhood. I was a young baby, living in a house on a platform in the jungle. My father was a priest. I felt very confused by what my father did for a living. I didn't know exactly what he did day after day and why he would sit still for hours on end, staring at a religious statue.

I went forward to another childhood scene. I was in a smoky room with several boys my age. We were facing older men who were cutting designs into our faces with sharpened stones. This event should have been painful but I was truly numb to the experience. Afterwards we were given a bitter-tasting liquid to drink and all of us felt very high. We were then told that we had now reached our manhood.

I could then see myself running full speed through a forest, chasing a deer. I was carrying a stick with an arrow on top of it. I finally ran this deer down and was able to throw the stick and hit the deer. The deer went down and I stooped to slit its throat. It made me feel reverent, happy, and very much like a man.

I moved forward and found myself in a house constructed of logs. I was there with my father who was explaining the principles of our religion. I loved and respected my father, but I was confused by all the talk of religion. My father explained to me that I am going to be the high priest of the tribe, which is a position that I didn't feel very well-suited to do.

This scene ended the flashback.

In the next scene I returned to the boat, watching this man being eaten by the fish. The crowd on the shore was wild with enthusiasm about the scene before them. I was gazing down at the man in the water, throwing in bits of leaves and bark. Clearly this act meant sacred things to the people on the shore but not to me. I performed the ceremony, but on the whole I was numb as to what it meant.

I flashed forward to the last day of my life. I walked into the village from the forest to see a tribe of wild men with feathers ravaging the village. I could see these people ripping down houses and beating people. My breath caught as I saw several men pull my wife from our hut and begin beating her. Then I just felt numb to the experience.

In the last scene I saw a man take a position in front of me. He had a bow and arrow and he raised it and let the arrow go. "This is it," I said to myself. I could see the arrow come at me in slow motion and stick in my chest. I saw it penetrate and rip my flesh. That was the end of my life.

I found it interesting that David's current life is such a cynical and areligious one, yet his regression was filled with spiritual search and questions about the meaning of various religious rites. He also shows anger at his father in the regression for not explaining his religion better in much the way that he was upset at his current-life father for not offering him spiritual guidance. David acknowledges a tremendous amount of spiritual quest in this regression.

The effect the regression had on him was to melt his cynicism about religious matters. He said he had long sought to deepen his spiritual side but the lack of guidance he had received in this area from his parents prevented him from really knowing what to do.

Another thing this regression contained was feelings of numbness when emotional responses would have been appropriate. I pointed this out to him and he once again referred to his upbringing. He said that because emotions were repressed in his family, he was rarely permitted to "feel" anything.

This regression cut to the very core of David's problems. In the fell swoop of a single regression, we were able to arrive at the very heart of the matters disturbing David.

BLOCKED BY THE PAST

A past-life therapist told me about a would-be author he was treating who was having "writer's block," that mental condition that prevents authors from putting pen to paper. It had become so bad for this writer that he was almost unable to write even a simple letter. That is when he sought the help of a regression therapist.

The therapist hypnotically regressed the patient and found his past life to be tightly linked to his problem.

I could see myself as though I were in a movie yet feel my feelings as though I were in the body I was looking at.

I was sitting by a window, writing. From the looks of my clothing and the fact that there were horse-drawn wagons in the street, I would guess the time period to be early nineteenth century.

The apartment I was in was a terrible place. It was dirty and small. Furniture was sparse. There was a single bed that took up one wall, the table, and the one chair that I was sitting on and that was it. Even with so little furniture, the place seemed crowded, so it must have been small. Out the window I could see rows of warehouses, so I have the idea that this place was in the warehouse district of some city.

Even though life was obviously tough, I was happy on this day. I was putting the finishing touches on a novel I had written. I had worked on this book for over a year now, and I was getting ready to give it to a publisher who had agreed to look at it.

I was excited. If I sold this to him, it would be a way out of my poverty. It would also mean that my chosen field would be accepted by my family, who thought I was wasting my time writing. I felt like this was my chance to prove them wrong.

In a later scene I was sitting at this same table looking out the window. I was very sad and bitter. The publisher said that my book was no good. He said that he didn't think it could ever be published. I didn't believe him. I took it to three other publishers and they said the same thing. I felt defeated and foolish.

In a late scene I was walking the streets. I am inside my body this time and my vision is blurred by tears. Another novel of mine has been rejected. I feel like killing myself but I can't do it. I swear I'll push on.

The last scene came late in my life. I could see myself from this third-person perspective. I had a balding head surrounded by a crown of gray hair. I was working in a library! I could see myself shuffling through cards. There were books all around my desk. I felt bitter. A thought came to mind: All of these books and not one of them has my name on it.

It is obvious to me that the patient has a fear of failure. His concern was that he would waste his life putting words on paper that would never be read. Since he had come to the past-life therapist to overcome writer's block, the therapist suggested that he place a time limit on success.

By that he meant that the writer should pursue a writing career for at least two years. If he didn't become reasonably successful in that time frame, he could then pursue other goals knowing that he had at least attempted his first love.

He took this suggestion to heart. He no longer felt the pressure to succeed, so his writer's block disappeared. And he did pursue a writing career for at least two years. After that he gave up the pen in favor of law school, feeling satisfied that he had at least given creative writing a try.

RESCRIPTING LIVES

A technique used by many past-life therapists is that of "rescripting" the past-life event. Simply stated, rescripting is the therapist's act of intervening at a critical point in the regression to change the experience. So, for instance, a person who fell to his death in a past life and now feared heights would rescript his regression experience so that death came naturally instead of at the hands of unforgiving gravity. In theory, that would help alleviate the fear of falling.

Rescripting has its roots in the work of the noted therapist Milton Erickson. He discovered it while he was conducting hypnotherapy with a patient who was afraid to have children because she feared that she would become as bad a parent as her own parents had been.

Instead of replacing her parents with more nurturing ones, Erickson added the memory of "the February Man," an imaginary friend of her father's. Through this new character, Erickson was able to inject the feelings of being loved and cherished. This helped the patient develop a stronger self-concept and eventually gave her the ability to rear children of her own.

Erickson doubted the validity of this technique himself, mainly because he questioned whether a therapist could successfully add experiences to a patient's life.

Despite his doubts about this technique, Erickson and others have used it with great success throughout the years. A technique known as "reparenting" is used by some therapists, in which the patient recalls bad childhood memories. The patient is then helped to become the hurt child through hypnosis or talking therapy. Then, while recalling those traumatic memories, the patient is told to reach out to his older self for the understanding and love that he needs. Richard Landis, a California psychologist, has used the reparenting technique with 60 percent of his patients over the last twenty years. He estimates that only 6 percent of those treatments failed.

Many past-life therapists feel that rescripting is necessary in many cases to have real impact on a person's current life. Although simply reliving a past life can be a catharsis in the way it releases emotions and helps the patient understand problems in his current life, some regression therapists think there must also be a change in the actual events of the past life.

In my own practice I don't use rescripting techniques. Patients I have tried it on have resisted efforts to change events. One patient said to me that the past-life experience itself seemed like a rescripting of her life. To go further than the regression itself required too great a leap for her logical mind. Other patients have said that they couldn't accept rescripting because the experiences were real and therefore could not be altered.

But the main reason I don't use rescripting is simply that I don't find it as effective as using the past-life discovery as a means to an end itself.

Past-life therapist Chet Snow wrote about a failed attempt at rescripting in *The Journal of Regression Therapy* (Vol III. Number 1, Spring 1988). In this account, the patient resists rescripting because the uncovered life "was supposed to end that way." However, the act of reliving this experience was therapy enough since the patient overcame the problem he had sought therapy for.

Here is Snow's case study:

> My first contact with the use of rescripting in a past-life context occurred "accidentally" some years ago, during advanced hypnotherapy training. As part of our preparation for certification, each of our class of about a dozen students was required to perform a (standard, current lifetime) hypnotic regression demonstration. Lacking a partner, one of the class—I'll call him Jim—asked the instructor to serve as his subject.
>
> The instructor, Jeff, readily agreed. The problem to be worked on concerned Jeff's frequent, inexplicable surges of anger and frustration while driving his rather antiquated and not-so-reliable automobile. Each time the car would refuse to start on cold mornings or stall out in traffic, Jeff found himself in a rage which was quite out of character. Normally he was a rather "cool" kind of guy, not easily perturbed. In fact, he explained that this situation had occurred just that morning and was therefore fresh in his mind. It seemed like an excellent case for a hypnotic regression. I should add that during previous sessions Jeff had informed us of his personal disbelief in the idea of reincarnation and of his dislike of past-life therapy.
>
> After a brief hypnotic induction, all was going fine in the regression until inexperienced Jim (a student therapist) asked the fatal open-ended question, "What is the origin behind these angry outbursts?" He then followed this by instructing Jeff to regress immediately to that original situation. He expected to find some repressed incident involving automobile traffic from Jeff's adolescence.
>
> Jeff paused momentarily and then, in a surprised and emotion-filled voice, began describing his situation as a

German soldier in the Libyan desert with Rommel's Afrikacorps. A tank driver, he found himself trapped inside a disabled, burning tank as British artillery shells exploded all around. As the tank lurched to a grinding halt, the soldier, obviously Jeff in his most recent past life, desperately tried to restart and move it and, when that failed, to escape—but the hatch was blocked. In a near panic he found himself cursing and clawing at the control panel, until the enemy artillery gunner found his range and ended the life in a violent explosion.

A couple of us who were familiar with past-life regressions had recognized what was going on and were, by this time, helping the thoroughly astonished student therapist get "Jeff" through this traumatic death incident and out of that mangled body. After he had made the transition to spirit and was in a much calmer, more detached position, Jim, the therapist, decided to apply what we had learned of rescripting in order to remove the incident and its consequences from Jeff's emotional makeup. He gave the standard suggestions that the part of Jeff holding on to this violent, frustrating scenario could now release it by changing the "memory" and altering the incident to a happier conclusion. As I recall, Jim specifically suggested that the tank could be made to start and move, thereby avoiding the fatal shell and allowing "Jeff" time to unblock the hatch and escape.

Despite this group's attempts to alter the outcome of this frightening and fatal event, Jeff wouldn't alter the circumstances. "It was supposed to end that way," he insisted. Nothing the therapists did would change that fact.

So it remained, until Snow hit upon an idea.

I suggested to Jim that he accept Jeff's viewpoint and ask him if he could release the fear and anger associated with the German tank death incident, explaining that he had no need to carry it over into current-life driving situations. Jeff readily accepted these ideas and allowed Jim to move him back up to the present, swiftly and easily. When Jeff emerged from the hypnosis he continued to deny that the incident represented memories from another lifetime, although he could not explain his reluctance to accept the rescripting suggestions. I noticed that he never again mentioned getting angry while driving.

Since this patient, Snow has gone on to use rescripting successfully.

There are some regression therapists—especially the reincarnationists—who don't believe that rescripting should be used at all. They feel that it is a quick fix that ignores the reasons for exploring past lives to begin with: to find the roots of the problem. They feel that past-life regressions offer the opportunity to see one's true self. If the true self isn't dealt with, the problems of this life will be the problems of the next one, and so on. A rescripted problem is one that is changed to suit the ego of a person's current life. Nonetheless, rescripting is a way of using past lives to solve current dilemmas.

THE REGRESSION TOOL

I am not trying to imply in this chapter that past-life regressions are a cure-all. Rather I am making the point that regression therapy may have an effect on some mental problems that therapists have never suspected.

By applying past-life regressions to many physical and mental illnesses, I have discovered one thing for sure: Regressions are *not* games. They are powerful tools for therapy.

III

—

What
Do
They
Mean?

5

Are Regressions Proof of Life Before Life?

Now that my attitude about past-life regressions has changed, I respond differently to questions about their meaning. The next three chapters are the best explanations I can offer about the meaning of regressions.

Which one do I believe? I do not believe in any single explanation. As you will see in these chapters, I have regressed dozens of patients and found that they can be fit neatly into the different categories of regression, even the one known as reincarnation.

Which brings up the most often asked question about past-life regressions: "Do these vivid recollections of some kind of past life represent reincarnation?"

ON ONE HAND . . .

That is always a tough question for me to answer. My scientific training and Christian rearing combine to evoke this response:

Reincarnation in no way jibes with Christian thought, with its reward and punishment system of heaven and hell. Instead reincarnation lends hope of renewal, with a life after life that hinges on the belief that beginnings come from the end, and so on.

Such belief is the antithesis of Christian thought. Most denominations believe in a physical death that will be reversed in the future when Christ returns and resurrects the righteous. As King Solomon said, "For the living know that they will die; but the dead know nothing . . ."

On the other hand, science says that we know nothing about what happens after death. Except for anecdotal accounts of people giving detailed descriptions of past lives, there is no *reproducible evidence* of life ever after. Reproducible evidence in the case of reincarnation and science would be the ability to prove that, say, white rats recently born had indeed lived before in the same laboratory.

Science has a tendency to accept only research that has reproducible results. That is fine if you are dealing with the effects of certain drugs on a population of people. Those results are observable.

But something like reincarnation poses certain obstacles to observation. Where does the soul go when it is between bodies? What is the evidence for a different plane of being where souls reside waiting for a physical incarnation? Why aren't we consciously aware of having lived before?

Such questions pose obstacles to scientific investigation because they are variables that would have to be eliminated before a "lab rat" study could be done.

So as a scientist influenced by a Christian upbringing I would have to say that past-life regressions are evidence of an altered state of the mind that is reached through hypnosis.

I am perfectly comfortable to let the matter rest there. Even though these experiences do not qualify as scientific proof of reincarnation, they are certainly proof of a rich and meaningful world beyond the conscious.

As we have already seen, regressions open a world that can affect our mental and physical well-being. This is also a world, as you will see in the next three chapters, that allows us the chance to explore a variety of lifestyles that we wouldn't normally be exposed to. It also gives us the chance to establish a myth about ourselves, one that keeps us on a chosen path or even explains to our deepest unconscious why we have chosen that path.

Past-life regressions can also help us tap a vast storehouse of knowledge that many of us don't even know we have. This is knowledge that is picked up randomly, or learned in school and "forgotten" (but really hidden in a fold of gray matter). The experience of tapping this knowledge is called "cryptomnesia" or "xenoglossia."

If I were to say that I was too much a scientist to believe in reincarnation, then I would also have to add that regressions are valuable because they can help people understand themselves. They can help us understand our fears, our desires, our hidden needs. They can justify us to ourselves. Because of that, past-life regressions are an enormously wonderful tool for self-discovery. They are a way of experimenting with various identities, modes of being, temperaments, personalities, and certainly a way of examining our psychological roots to explore the type of person we are.

Where does this stream of images that we tap come from? And what is its purpose? This wellspring of imagery is one of the enduring mysteries of the mind. But thankfully its benefits are readily available.

. . . ON THE OTHER HAND

But that still doesn't answer the question: "Do past-life regressions represent proof of reincarnation?"

As a worldly realist I would reply, "maybe." To begin with, the person who thinks reincarnation is a belief held by only a few wrong-thinking people has probably lived life with blinders on. Reincarnation is possibly the oldest and most widely held spiritual belief known to mankind. It isn't just a belief held by ancient religions, but by current ones as well. And believers in survival of the soul aren't just in India or other exotic countries, but probably work and live right next to you.

In fact, one of the world's great reincarnation researchers is Ian Stevenson, a professor of psychiatry at the University of Virginia. Stevenson examines "cases suggestive of reincarnation" by offering detailed descriptions and analyses of the cases he has uncovered. He then presents all the details of the case on a table, and next to it the names of people used to cross-check the information presented in the case. These tables can go on for several pages, and serve to show the painstaking detail that is involved in examining each case.

One such case was that of Parmod Sharma, born in 1944 to the family of a professor living in Uttar Pradesh, India. As Stevenson wrote:

> When he was about two and a half, he began to tell his mother not to cook because he had a wife in Moradabad who could cook. Later, between the ages of three and four, he began to refer to a large soda and biscuit shop which he said he had in Moradabad. He asked to go to Moradabad. He said he was one of the "Mohan Brothers." He claimed to be well-to-do and to have had another shop in Saharanpur. He showed an extraordinary interest in biscuits and shops. . . . He related how in the previous life he had become ill after eating too much curd and said he had "died in a bathtub."

Stevenson traveled to India to interview the child. Then he talked to the family and learned that they had no previous knowledge or friendship with anyone named "Mohan." Stevenson then found that there was a biscuit shop in Moradabad known as the Mohan Brothers. He found that they owned another biscuit shop in Saharanpur. He also discovered the existence of a brother who had died of a gastrointestinal illness. Did he die in a bathtub? Close.

> The witnesses of the Mehra family stated that Parmanand tried a series of naturopathic bath treatments when he had appendicitis. He had some of these treatments during the days just before his death but did not actually die in a bathtub. In a letter dated September 7, 1949, Sri B.L. Sharma stated that Parmod had said he died of being "wet with water" and that he (Sri B.L. Sharma) had learned (presumably from the Mehra family) that Parmanand had been given a bath immediately before his death.

Stevenson has researched dozens of reincarnation cases around the world. Although his research is anecdotal, it is heavily researched so that it doesn't rely strictly on the word of the person having the experience.

Stevenson's meticulous work in the field of reincarnation has helped the subject receive some serious consideration by his scientific colleagues. Said one noted researcher: "[Stevenson's work has] moved us further along the path of what might be called the direct approach to the issue. Such approaches tackle the problem head on, seeking evidence for the existence of surviving personality patterns . . . it makes survival a researchable issue worthy of a valid place on a scientific agenda."

Does Stevenson's work prove that the soul goes on and on, from one body to the next? Not in a "scientific" sense. But it does offer evidence that is hard to ignore, even in a skeptical world.

SOME CASES DIFFICULT TO IGNORE

All of the past-life regressions presented in this book could easily represent reincarnation experiences. Skeptics say no, that they are representative of a dissociated mental state, or are simply the result of the subject trying to please the hypnotist.

Such an argument may please the skeptic, but it does little to convince the person who looks deeper. How is it, for instance, that a person can create such vividly detailed lives? Dr. Helen Wambach, a past-life researcher, found that 90 percent of the people who attempted hypnotic regression were able to recall events from a previous life. How is it that their "past lives" can seem as real as their current ones? On the surface one can say that these are flights of fantasy. But why are the flights so vivid? And why don't most of them seem like fantasy?

These are questions that make past-life regressions a puzzle, even for regression therapists. In talking to other regression therapists I frequently find that they too are unable to determine whether hypnotic regressions really represent reincarnation or just the active unconscious mind at work (or play).

As one therapist put it: "Just when you almost believe that

regressions are only the work of the unconscious, along comes a case that has evidence of a person's previous life. Then you swing the other way."

THE REBORN NOBLEMAN

One such case is that of Dr. Paul Hansen, a past-life therapist in Colorado. In a personal discussion Dr. Hansen told me how he was regressed in 1981 and found himself as a French nobleman named Antoine Poirot. He knew that he lived on an estate outside Vichy, France. His wife's name was Marie and they had two children.

He was the "ruler" of an area about the size of a large county in the western United States. From a small château he directed hundreds of peasants through their duties.

"The most specific scene in the regression was one in which I was riding with my wife through well-manicured woods up to the château," recalled Hansen. "She had on a bright red dress made of velvet and was riding sidesaddle."

Not only was Hansen able to recall his name but he also had a date in the 1600s. With date and name he was able to search the birth certificate records handed down through the centuries. He was able to find record of Poirot's birth as it was recorded by a parish priest.

Hansen has no recollection of ever having seen or having heard this name before "remembering" it during the regression. Nor is there any reason that this wealthy farmer in 1600s France would appear in European history books. Hansen feels that this experience is proof that he lived before.

This wouldn't be enough proof for the scientific community, but for him it is plenty.

DONNER PARTY REVISITED

This case study comes from Dick Sutphen, noted hypnotist and regression therapist. Several years ago he regressed a German woman who was having trouble controlling her weight. She was on a cycle of fasting/binging and hoped that Sutphen could help her improve her eating habits. In the course of the regression, she found herself as a member of the Donner Party, those ill-fated travelers trapped in the Rockies during a blizzard with nothing to eat but the members of their own group.

Was her experience a reincarnation event? Read the transcript of the regression and Sutphen's comments and decide for yourself.

Dick: Speak up and tell me what you perceive . . . what's happening?

Eva: I am afraid. (She begins to tremble.)

Dick: What are you afraid of?

Eva: Of a trap, in the snow. All of us. We didn't get out before it snowed.

Dick: Are you with others? How many?

Eva: Oh, maybe thirty or forty others.

Dick: Okay, tell me everything you can about the situation.

Eva: We were trying to get through before the snow came. We didn't make it. Now we're stuck. We can't get out.

Dick: What was your mode of transportation?

Eva: Wagon and walking.

Dick: How old are you?

Eva: I am ten.

Dick: What's your name?

Eva: Mary.

Dick: All right, Mary. You're ten years of age, you're trapped with thirty or forty others. Were you part of a wagon train? Is that it?

Eva: Yes.

Dick: Okay, tell me about what's happening now. Tell me more about it.

Eva: Well, we . . . it's very cold, and we have nothing to eat.

Dick: Okay, what was the name of your group?

Eva: Uh, Donner?

Dick: Yes. Okay, I want you to move forward to something very important on the count of three: one, two, three.

Eva: My grandfather died. He just died.

Dick: Is your mother there? Your father, are they there?

Eva: My father is not here.

Dick: Your father, where's your father?

Eva: I think he was waiting for us on the other side . . . I don't know.

Dick: All right, you were traveling with your mother and your grandfather, is that correct?

Eva: Yeah, and my sister, and my brothers and Grandfather died.

Dick: What is your mother telling you? Will you bury your grandfather?

Eva: Well, we don't say, we don't say that. They're feeding us now, they're feeding us now.

Dick: They're feeding you.

Eva: And they don't want us to know it's Grandfather. I just know it is. I just know it is, and I shouldn't be eating this. (Eva is shaking and tears are rolling down her cheeks.)

Dick: Are you hungry, Mary?

Eva: Yeah.

Dick: Very, very hungry? I want you to experience the hunger. How does it feel to be that hungry?

Eva: It doesn't matter. Nothing matters.

Dick: Yes it does matter. You're eating. You're hungry and it hurts. Tell me about it. I want you to totally experience this. You're going to experience it and you're going to come out the other side. (Additional time taken to experience the hunger.) Now tell me, what's it feel like to be this hungry?

Eva: It's awful! Your own brother and sister become your enemies, that's all it is, is hunger. Nothing else, there's nothing else.

Dick: All right, we're going to move forward now. Mary, you're moving deeper into the winter. Tell me what is happening now.

Eva: More older people are disappearing.

Dick: They are disappearing, or they're dying? What's happening to the older people?

Eva: I don't think they're just dying anymore. I think, I think the others are killing them.

Dick: You think they're killing the old people to eat them?

Eva: I think . . . I really think so, yes.

Dick: All right. Time . . . how is your time spent? What do you do with your day? I want to know everything that's happening.

Eva: Inside of a hole, inside of a snow hole.

Dick: A snow hole, okay.

Eva: We just huddle together because it is very cold.

Dick: So this is how you spend your entire day? Huddling together to keep warm?

Eva: Children, their mothers and others.

Dick: How? Do you live individually, or are you in one encampment? How is it set up? How many of you are left now, and how is it set up?

Eva: Well, there are just two families left. But it's not all one family in the hole. It's mostly just children and the women left. And I think everybody knows now, everybody knows now except the very little ones. I shouldn't be eating this.

Dick: And you are eating. What do you feel about eating the people?

Eva: I think it's awful.

Dick: And you're doing it. What do you feel about doing it when you think it's awful? (I purposely push her to cause her to release repressed emotions.)

Eva: Part of me thinks it's all right, and part of me thinks it's not. And mother says it's all right.

Dick: Okay, I want you to move forward in time a little further, a little further, Mary. More time is passing, deeper and deeper into the winter. What's happening now?

Eva: There aren't too many left. Just the women and children. Two men.

Dick: Two men?

Eva: And they're afraid of the women. They have a hole by themselves.

Dick: The men have their own hole, because they're afraid of the women?

Eva: Yeah.

Dick: Why are they afraid of the women?

Eva: I guess they want to keep their children alive.

Dick: The women want to keep their children alive, what does that mean?

Eva: They will want the men . . . to eat them. (She begins to cry and shudder.)

Dick: Let go of this now, and without pain or emotion, on the count of three, I want you to move now to the very last day of your life in this past life we're now examining. You will not have died, you will not have crossed over into spirit. But it's now the last day of your life, and I want you to tell me what's happening.

Eva: I am now a grandmother and I'm old.

Dick: Well, Mary, I want you to look back on your life and tell me about what happened. You were trapped as part of the Donner party in the snow. So you escaped, is this correct?

Eva: Yeah. Spring . . . spring came.

Dick: Spring came and you survived. How many survived?

Eva: Not many, not too many. Fifteen? Twenty?

Dick: And you went on and lived. Where did you live your life, Mary?

Eva: We moved far away and changed our name.

Dick: Why did you change your name?

Eva: People. People knew.

Dick: People knew that the survivors of the Donner party ate other people?

Eva: Yes.

Dick: And condemned them for it?

Eva: Yes.

Dick: And what did you feel about that? What did you feel in being one of the survivors of that wagon train, and having eaten the people? Is this something you dealt with all your life?

Eva: I felt I never wanted to eat meat again, never. That I always knew it was wrong.

Dick: It was wrong to eat the people.

Eva: Yeah, I shouldn't have eaten any of them.

Dick: You were a ten-year-old child, and your momma told you it was all right. Did that not make any difference? You still felt it was really wrong?

Eva: My grandfather, especially. Especially him. Yeah. It was wrong.

Dick: Did your brother and sister survive, Mary?

Eva: Yeah. But they all moved away. We never wanted to talk to each other after that.

Dick: You never wanted to talk to each other?

Eva: No. We all moved different ways, and lost contact. We just didn't want anybody to know us, we didn't even want to know each other.

Dick: Did anyone ever know again? Your husband?

Eva: No.

Dick: You never told him?

Eva: No. I never told anybody.

Dick: So, this is something you've repressed your entire life. Was this not a terrible burden, Mary?

Eva: It still is. I still feel it. I'm afraid to die.

Dick: Why are you afraid to die?

Eva: I'm afraid to see my grandfather.

Dick: Tell me about that.

Eva: If there is a heaven and hell, he might come back.

Dick: Do you think he is going to blame a little ten-year-old girl? He might have felt good about the fact that he was able to help keep you alive. Don't you think that is possible?

Eva: I'm just afraid to find out. I don't know. My mother always told me that, what you say.

Dick: She told you what?

Eva: That it didn't matter. That he had died anyway.

Dick: After you were grown, did you also lose contact with your mother?

Eva: No. She died after that. She never got well again.

Dick: She never got well after the winter?

Eva: No. She didn't. I don't think she wanted to live anymore after that.

Dick: What about your father? Was he waiting for you on the other side of the mountain or not?

Eva: No. I think he disowned us when he found out. I don't know.

In follow-up research, Sutphen found that Eva had come to our country in 1953 and never studied U.S. history. She had no conscious memory of ever having heard of the Donner tragedy of 1846.

In researching the actual incident, Sutphen found that there were a total of eighty-seven people who tried to cross the Rockies on that fateful voyage. Two sections of that wagon train reached what is now known as Donner Lake where they were able to build two crude log cabins. The third section, led by George Donner, was caught far from the rest of the group. They abandoned their wagons and pitched tents that they reinforced with ox skins. Twelve-foot drifts forced them to dig holes to the top of the snow, just as Eva had described.

From the three wagon train sections, forty-seven survived, mostly women and children. Among those who were separated from the rest of the group, eight survived, two of them men.

CONCLUSION

The cases presented in this chapter—and indeed the entire book—all present the possibility of reincarnation. Where did these "memories" come from if not a previous life? Why do they have such profound effects on some people if they don't represent "real" events? The questions can go on and on.

Unfortunately the answer to the reincarnation question—Are we born again and again?—doesn't exist. Science can only say that it can't be proven, while anecdotal evidence says that it can't be disproven.

The result is a question that each individual must answer for him- or herself.

6

Present Lessons from Past Lives

We are all mysteries to ourselves.

From the viewpoint of other people, most of us seem calm. We go about our daily chores in a perfectly logical fashion; eating, working, sleeping in much the same way every day. But beneath that calm exterior is an upheaval of activity, a constant churning of thoughts and ideas; of fantasized feats and subliminal beliefs. On any given day we spend much more time talking to ourselves than we do to other people. We question ourselves, bolster our egos, daydream about distant lands and various lifestyles.

In the same way that we tend to repeat ourselves in conversation with other people, so are conversations with ourselves recalled again and again by our deepest companion, the subconscious.

The subconscious is the great creator and the great experiencer. It can take the things that we daydream about and run with them. It can help us dream about what it is like to be the Prince of Wales or a cop on the beat. It can be an imaginative means of exploring feelings that we don't understand, a sort of exploration of alter ego.

When its creativity is tapped by hypnosis, it can take us on magical tours even more vivid than our daydreams. Sometimes these tours go to places we didn't consciously know we wanted to go.

One time I regressed a very macho man only to find he was a homosexual in a past life. The experience was a shock to him and somewhat of an embarrassment.

I suspect, however, that he had been subconsciously curious about this lifestyle. When under hypnosis, he felt relaxed enough to explore those feelings freely. As a result of this new exploration, he became less biased and more understanding toward gays.

Another time, I regressed a very puritanical and bookish woman of thirty. Her entire life had been directed toward education and her credentials reflected that fact. She had three master's degrees and was working on another at the time of this regression.

Before I regressed her we talked. Her life was beginning to bother her, she said. Because of her parents' bad marriage she had ignored the opposite sex, thinking of any relationship as a bad one. She had never made attempts to look attractive. Instead, she tried to do just the opposite, concealing her feminine ways under masculine attire. She rarely went outside her studies for activity, choosing instead to spend most of her time "with my nose buried in a book."

Now she wanted to break through this self-imposed wall. She had never had an in-depth relationship with a man, but was wondering if such a relationship would necessarily turn out as bad as that of her parents. She was even thinking that she might like to have children.

She was vague about why she wanted to be regressed, but said that she wanted to see if there was anything in a past life that had led to her current feeling of isolation.

What came up in the regression was not a memory of a bad relationship. Quite the contrary. The regression became a way of exploring her deepest curiosities. Here is what happened.

> I went back to a life, but I have no idea where it was. I think it was somewhere like Scandinavia. There was no sense of a date, but I am sure that it was many hundreds of years ago. We had no metal. Life here was very Stone Age.
>
> In one scene I was sitting by a campfire watching my husband put tiny arrowheads on the tips of sticks with glue made of pitch from a tree. He then bound them with a real tough cord. At another point I found myself looking

at an animal hide. It was stretched between two logs. I was scraping it with a flint blade. I found myself really working hard on this hide and enjoying the repetition of my work.

At some points I could see myself. I had very whitish gray hair. I was wearing a tunic that was made from a roughly hewn material. I remember looking into the eyes of my husband, too, and seeing eyes that were deep, deep blue.

In this life I had at least eight children. I had affection for all of these kids, although in that culture there was a sense of a cooperative unit, that everyone in the society took a role in raising them.

I guess I loved my husband, but I really thought of us more as a unit than in terms of lovers. We depended upon each other to exist. There really was no romantic attraction.

I remembered times of great joy. In one scene we were all running around on a summer day, chasing each other and playing keep-away with some object that we were throwing back and forth.

At another point, I saw my husband killed. We were getting into a boat on this rapidly moving river when he suddenly fell backwards into the water and was swept away. I ran back to the camp and got my son who was in his early teenage years and he ran down the river to find him. He found him dead.

I was able to watch the funeral. There were a bunch of friends who came over. They hollowed out a tree trunk and put his body inside. I dressed him in a new leather outfit and put a bone scraper in the hollowed-out tree with him. They sang and wept and then we all carried the body to a place near our lodge and buried him.

I was devastated by his death. Not only would I miss him, but there were practical considerations, too. It was extremely cold here, and we needed all the help we could get in the gathering and hunting of food and supplies. Also the area was very sparsely populated. There was no chance that I could find another partner unless one of the women died and her husband suddenly became available.

The very last thing I could remember was climbing up a rocky hill with my children. That's the last thing I remember, that and having a fading feeling of wonder at what would happen to my children. I guess I must have died at that point.

It immediately struck me that this was a polar opposite life from the one she had been living. Where she had been independent and intellectual all of her life, in her regression she was very fecund and dependent. Where she had really lived apart from the earth, she relied upon it in her regression.

She was amazed at what the regression found. The life she experienced was completely opposite from the one she now lived—and certainly from the one she expected to find in a hypnotic regression. She had not expected this kind of regression, since being an "earth mother" was hardly an image that occupied her conscious thoughts. I reminded her that there are feelings held deep within us that we often don't understand or wish to explore on a conscious level.

Here are other cases that make me believe that past-life regressions can be a forum for the expression of alter ego.

QUESTIONING AUTHORITY

Mike is the son of a small-town mayor and a law student who is anxious to begin his own practice. He is quick to admit that he respects authority and even plans to become part of the political system some day.

There is no history of drug or alcohol abuse in his family and Mike himself drinks very little. I bring these up—authority and alcohol—because his regression contained so much abuse of these two factors.

I was plainly in Europe. I think it was about 200 to 300 years ago but I have no idea exactly when or where. I think it was in Great Britain. I was a little boy. I was walking through the streets at night and I remember being appalled at the number of homes in which alcohol was being consumed. As I walked down the street and looked in windows, it seemed as though there was someone drinking in every living room.

I remember being very worried. My mother and father were about thirty and as I came up to the apartment we lived in, I could see that we lived in squalor. The apartment was small and had gray walls. My mother was very obsessed with religion and all the walls were covered with pictures of Jesus and the Virgin Mary.

My parents were drunk all the time. I had a great feeling of desperation as I entered the apartment. I looked down the streets and the scene was frightening. There were drunk people lying all over the streets. There were terrible sanitation conditions all around, with the gutters being used as sewers for human waste. The city was a horrible mess.

One thing that impressed me in this life was the great difficulty that people had in communicating with one another. Without telephones it seems incredibly tough. There were several times in which I noticed other people being sent to fetch someone else or to deliver a hand-written message. These couriers were doing the job of the telephone!

The one incident that brought the difficulty of communications home to me was seeing a man hit by a horse and carriage. A flock of people gathered around and someone was sent to fetch a doctor. It seemed to take forever before the doctor got there.

This place was very noisy. It was also inhabited by disease-ridden people who were walking around with all kinds of terrible illnesses.

In the next scene, I found myself in a church at about twelve years of age. I felt terribly alone and had the feeling that my parents had died. I had left the city and was in this church asking the minister if there was any sort of help I could get. The minister was a thin, pale, sickly looking man. He didn't give me any real guidance, only biblical platitudes. At that point in my life, I had the feeling that the authorities didn't know any more about things than I did.

I then moved forward a few years. I found myself working as a shoemaker's apprentice in a small town. The shop was very dark and down some stairs from the street. In this shop I was flooded with the smell of leather. The shoemaker I worked for was a very happy man. He had a twelve-year-old son who was also learning the trade and a daughter who came in occasionally to visit.

The wife was a kind woman who loved to cook for us.

At this point I went forward. I had married a woman that I met at a carnival. We moved to another town and were setting up a shoe store of our own. This was a pleasant village and I became an important part of this town.

Again I went forward and could see myself in excruciating pain. I could see myself from a distance. I don't know what the source of the pain was, but I could see that my wife was alarmed and didn't know what to do.

She took me to a doctor who could answer none of our questions about this pain. To me, this doctor was similar to the minister I met as a child. He was pompous and didn't really know anything about what he was talking about.

A few days after leaving the doctor's office I could see myself holding my abdomen and grimacing with pain. I could see beads of sweat clearly on my head. It was obviously more pain than I could bear.

I saw a scene in which the doctor recommended surgery and I knew I had no other choice. I could see myself and my wife in a carriage headed for the hospital. I was very ill and worried and the sight of the hospital didn't help very much. It was a big, dreary institution with wrought-iron gates.

Finally, I found myself in an operating room that was amazingly dreary by modern standards. There didn't seem to be an effort to keep it clean, although I didn't see this as being anything to be concerned about at the time since the cleanliness standards in those days were quite different. What was on my mind was my wife and her security if I were to die.

As I lay on this table and looked up, I saw the doctor's coat stained with blood. There was no anesthetic. I was tied to the table and told to remain as calm as possible. Then he began to cut me down by my stomach.

I felt myself being cut by a crude instrument. There was terrible pain and then no feeling at all. I felt myself out of my body and I went over to my wife, who was there in the room. I couldn't communicate with her. I couldn't communicate with anyone. I finally just felt myself wandering off into a bright light.

There were several obvious questions to be asked from this regression: Was Mike the child of an alcoholic? Were there alcoholics in his immediate family? Did he dislike authority?

The answer to all of these questions was "no." There were no alcoholics in his family. In fact, when I asked about the role of alcohol in his family he said that his parents didn't even allow it in the house. No one in the family drank. They are all hard-core Methodists and set on the belief that alcohol doesn't have a place in the home.

His parents are very rigid and compulsive, almost cleanliness buffs, the way he described them. His father is a small-town mayor who expects Mike to be a doctor or a lawyer.

Mike has the same expectations of himself. Also, his appearance is always meticulous and his bearing is that of a very orderly person.

I find it interesting that his past-life regression has an uncontrolled and untidy environment. It is really the antithesis of what he is in this life. Also, there are two points in this regression in which he shows disdain for authority. One when he asks the priest for help and receives only platitudes, and the other in which he gets no straight answers from his doctor about his illness. This happens despite his respect for authority in his "current" life.

All of this combined makes me think that Mike is exploring an alternative lifestyle. Nothing in his regression is like his current life. His parents are drunks who ignore him in this regression. In his real life, his parents are very sober and controlling.

Being the son of a politician exposes him to a lot of authority. However, much of the authority he is exposed to stems only from positioning for political power, not necessarily from a sense of what is right or wrong. As a result, Mike sees many authorities as being persuasive "know-nothings."

Also there is a communications problem indicated here by the difficulty people have in reaching one another without telephones. I think this relates clearly to his own difficulty in getting through to his parents about his feelings.

A LIFE OF REPRESSION

Brooke is a heterosexual woman with no expressed desire to experiment sexually with other women. She has a steady boyfriend and is happy with that arrangement.

On the family front, she has always been encouraged by her well-educated father and socially active mother to live life to its fullest. That is why the results of her regression were such a surprise to me.

I was a young woman on a farm. I was able to walk up on a ridge and look down on the farmhouse. Around the outside of it in the front yard were my brothers and sisters. In one sense I felt that I belonged to the farm, but on the other hand I needed to get out and explore and study the world.

I moved forward and found myself with my mother, father, and the other kids. I was listening intently to my father. I can't remember the words but I had a sense that he was talking about nature in an almost worshipful way.

As we ate, he was telling us that this food was brought about by the interaction of man with the earth. He was telling us that this process of farming enabled us to eat.

He was a religious person, almost a visionary type.

Mother, on the other hand, was hardly apparent. She was a mousy figure. No matter how hard I tried in these regressions, I never got a clear picture of her. The clearest picture I got was seeing her in the background sewing clothing.

I moved forward to my teenage years. I was in my father's study. In addition to being a farmer, my father was a real reader. He would spend a considerable amount of time in his study with his books. I was curious about that world. I wanted to learn how to read and that presented a problem to him. His attitude was that girls did not need to be poking around in literature. He thought I should be in the sewing room learning mother's work.

I was very upset. Here I was a teenager who was getting no formal education at all. Yet I had a strong desire to wade into my father's book world. I was over-whelmed with sadness when I looked at those books. I knew that I didn't want to be raised in the image of my mother. I wanted to be like my father.

I went forward a few years. I was in a moderate-sized city where I had been sent by my family to become a governess. The farm had fallen on hard times and my parents had to get rid of all the kids they could.

I was a governess to two children whose father was a businessman involved in the selling of some kind of insurance. The wife was much younger than her husband.

At this point in my life I felt very much like a male. Because of that, I had many conflicts about my sexuality. Deep down I was very troubled about this. I felt like a freak and was sure that nobody else could have the kind of feelings I was having. The sexual identity conflict hung over me all of my life, but it became a real problem in living with this couple.

It was with them that I discovered I wasn't alone in being attracted to the same sex.

One day in the parlor, the lady of the house made a sexual advance on me. The children were gone and she suggested that we should "experiment." Of course, I was interested right away, since I didn't think anyone else even thought such a thing was a possibility.

I don't remember how long the lady and I had this affair, but I do remember when my stay at their house ended.

One day I was alone with the husband and he suggested that we get to know each other better. I resisted and he insisted. He put his arm around me and tried to get me to sit on the couch with him. That was it. I packed my belongings and left that very day.

After that I was lost. It was almost like I was crazy. I wandered the town in a daze for a long time. I lived on the streets or in worn-out rooming houses until my money dwindled away.

Finally I decided I couldn't deal with these problems of my questionable sexuality. I decided to end my life. One night I went out and jumped off a bridge into the river that ran through this town.

That is how I died.

As I have already established, her actual life is not in any way so dramatic. She is not a lesbian and is in fact very close to her boyfriend. They have been going together for two years and have an active sexual life.

She has many girlfriends that she has been affectionate with over the years, but never in a sexual way.

Her family is far from being a farm family. Her father is a physician with a wonderful sense of humor who has always encouraged her to pursue learning of all kinds. Her mother is an active person in the community, a pillar in the local women's political group, and has organized many popular civic functions.

Why did she identify with a male in this regression?

Why did she have sex with another woman?

Why was she so repressed by her father in this past life?

Why did her mother in the regression have virtually no identity?

Once again, I think the regression was an opportunity to explore an alternative lifestyle.

Psychiatric theory says that all of us have homosexual leanings, each and every person. Brooke has led a life of clear identification with the feminine role. This regression is her way of "testing the waters," of seeing what life is like for a polar opposite personality.

WARM LIFE IN THE COLD COUNTRY

The same is true of Bill, a former clergyman who left his ministry after concluding that he was gay. He studied at several major Bible colleges and was rising in the conference hierarchy before deciding to resign.

Because of his homosexuality, he was very surprised at the content of his regression, which found him as a heterosexual in an ancient Indian tribe. But as with Brooke, I saw Bill's regression as a means of examining an alternative lifestyle.

I came out in the middle of an arctic wasteland! I was a member of an Eskimo tribe.

I was able to look down at what I was wearing and saw that I had on a parka made of animal skins. Still it was so cold where I was that I could even feel the chill on my face during the regression.

In one of the first scenes, I was out fishing in a small boat. I was not catching anything, but I wasn't too distressed by it. I just leaned back and drank in the beautiful blue sky that looked even bluer in contrast to the snowy ground. I felt a great sense of peace in this environment.

I skipped to a scene in which I found myself in a village. This wasn't an igloo village as I would have expected. Rather, it was a village of shacks, sort of dug into the ground.

I went into my house. There I saw my wife. In the context of my current life, it surprises me that I was married. But in the regression, I wasn't surprised at all. I clearly felt the love of a husband for this woman. Let me describe her. She looked surprisingly western to me. She had long black hair and skin that was a little lighter than the other women in the tribe. Her cheekbones were higher and overall her facial features were much more angular than the other women.

Everyone in this culture was very cheerful and friendly. There was a great sense of cooperation among the people. We all did things together like cleaning and sharing our catches. There was a sense that it was us against nature. Although nature was beautiful during this season, we all knew she could become savage. For us to bicker for any reason made no sense and we all seemed to know that. It would have just taken precious time and we needed all of that to prepare for winter.

I felt the same sense of great cooperation with my wife. This cooperation was fun, but it was definitely geared to survival in this sometimes hostile environment. Overall, I think we all realized that we held the balance as to whether we would survive or not.

I saw my wife and me in several different scenes. In one we were huddled together underneath piles of animal skins as a winter storm raged outside the house. It was a brutal storm, but still we managed to stay warm and enjoy each other's company at the same time.

In another scene, we were fitting animal skins together to make clothing. The feeling was one of happiness and contentment as we tried to figure out how to fit these seal skins together to make a good coat.

I loved this woman very much. It was wonderful being with her in this environment of great natural beauty. Since this regression, I have a great sense of longing to get back to her. I know I have to find this woman because we were certainly soulmates in this past

life. I also am sure that we will find each other, that
we are meant to be together.

Given our physical and psychological makeup, the results of
Bill's regression were less surprising to me than they were to him. I
pointed out to him that even in the gayest of men, there is
curiosity about the heterosexual lifestyle. The reverse is true too:
The most macho of men wonder about the gay life. I saw this as
his way of harmlessly exploring the hetero world.

BOBBY'S WALK ON THE WILD SIDE

Bobby's father is in air force intelligence, and as a result the
family has traveled all over the world. He has two younger sisters
who, from the pictures he has shown me, resemble the blonde,
perky, cheerleader type.

Bobby is compulsively meticulous, with every hair in place.
He dresses fastidiously and proudly declares himself to be "hyper-
organized."

I mention these traits because in Bobby's regression, he
seems to be making peace with the wild side of life. Rather
than finding himself in a white lab coat working with "something scientific and clean," as he expected, Bobby found himself in a completely different environment. Here is what he
experienced.

I was in a meadow high in the mountains. I was a very
young child, somewhere between three and five. I was walking very quietly as though I was sneaking up on something.

There were other people around me in this scene and
I was surprised at the way they looked. They had larger,
more bulbous heads than people in my current life. Also,
they had much less hair than I would have expected on
ancient people who lived in a colder climate. I had the
realization that this was very ancient history, somewhere
in the beginning of mankind.

We were walking toward a shelter that overlooked a

river. The field in front of us was covered with acres of beautiful flowers.

I flashed to a scene where I was lying in front of a shelter listening to the chirping of bugs. I looked around at my shelter. There were posts dug into the ground. On top of the posts were piles of debris like tree limbs and animal skins.

I went forward and could see a huge woolly animal. At this point I was very panicked. I wanted to run away and get away from this thing. I felt myself running down a hill and then I faded into another scene.

In this one, we were gathered around a fruit tree. There were about ten of us, and from my perspective in this current life I had the feeling that these creatures could just barely be defined as people. We were standing around this tree, looking at the fruit that hung above our heads. I wanted to pick a piece of it but I didn't. I think I was waiting for someone else to do it instead of me.

In one scene I felt myself falling down this hill, with rocks and dirt coming loose and falling down around me. I rolled and rolled for what seemed like forever. When I stopped at the bottom and came out of the stupor that taking a beating leaves one in, I found myself looking into the faces of two of these misshapen and ugly creatures. They were very frightened about my bad fall and were clearly concerned that I had been hurt. They were happy to see me get up and move around under my own power.

We were all very nervous at night. In one scene, the leader of our group kept going to the opening of the shelter and peering out nervously. The rest of us huddled together, afraid of what might be out there waiting for us. I had the sense that sometime in the past, a member of the tribe had gone out into the darkness and had never returned. Since then, we all believed that the darkness ate people.

In another scene I was very young, looking down into a valley at a herd of animals. These were animals we had never seen before. They looked like what we know as buffalos. I wanted to keep watching these animals but the rest of the tribe had no curiosity. They just moved on.

On the last day of my life, I was walking along feeling very sick. I had a bad fever and couldn't keep up with the members of the tribe as they searched for food. Finally I just lay down in a field. The tribe members picked me up and carried me back to the shelter. They fed me and kept me comfortable but their feeble efforts did no good. Over the course of several days I became weaker and weaker. My fever became worse and my fear greater because I didn't know what was happening. I finally just heaved an enormous sigh and died.

The last thing I saw from this life was the tribe members piling sticks and leaves on top of my body.

Bobby was somewhat puzzled by the content of this regression but its purpose became quite clear. This experience gave him the opportunity to discover what life with no control was like.

He appreciated that chance and also liked the thought that such wildness was inside of him somewhere.

THE WOMANLY KEN

Ken is a very athletic young man who lives in a big city and works in his family's insurance business. He has a healthy heterosexual love life and clearly identifies heavily with the male point of view.

I highlight these issues of sex because Ken's regression took him back to a life in which he was a woman. Here is his story.

I was plainly a woman in this regression.

In the first scene, I was wrapped in a blanket and being carried down a steep mountain by my mother. I could see the green mountains and the stark gray peaks off in the distance.

We were moving down a slope and across a rushing mountain stream. We were heading toward our house, a big structure with flat stones, a flat roof, and big wooden beams. I was being carried somewhat precariously by my mother but I had no fear. I sensed that she had been over this path many times before and I felt very confident of safety in her grasp.

Despite this feeling of safety I was crying as we walked to the house. My mother had big red dots on her face that looked awful and were frightening to me.

In this scene my mother was clothed in a very dark dress with colorful beads in her hair. She was happy despite my tears and was cheerily singing a song.

In another scene I was running very fast down the mountain. My grandfather was coming. I could see him coming up the road and I couldn't wait to reach him because he always had candy for me in the pockets of his robe. This candy seems to be honey, sugar, and nuts all rolled up in a ball. When he gave it to me, I popped it into my mouth and tried to chew it all at once. He laughed at me as I wrestled with this big mouthful of sticky candy.

I looked past my grandfather and could see my father working down in the valley. It seemed as though he was always working and his work paid off. The fields below us were covered with green squares of land that were culti-vated by his hand.

I could see myself at the age of twelve. I was sitting beside a loom being taught weaving by my mother. That was a fleeting image. Then I went forward to the age of fourteen and could see myself standing by a road looking at strangers who had come from far, far away. I was very excited by the strangers because it was the first time I had any realization of a world beyond the valley.

These men were very dark-skinned. One of them reached into a pocket and gave me a comb for my hair. They then took a machine out of their possessions and wound it up. It was an old phonograph player that played the sound of a man singing. When I heard this, I fell down on the ground and began laughing uncontrollably.

I just laughed and laughed and told them that this was magic.

I moved forward to my married life. I saw my wedding day and felt the feelings of happiness as I was joined with my husband. We were dancing together at our wedding party which was being held outside my family's home in that beautiful mountain valley. I could sense that we would be living the lives of farmers. Very vaguely I could sense that I would be having children in the near future.

I moved forward to the day of my death. There were swellings all over my body, especially under my arms and on my stomach. I was sweating and hot. I could see my husband crying and could feel all of my children around me. The last thing I remembered was trying to console my husband. He was grief-stricken that he would have to go through life without me.

What was this one about? It is truly a mystery to me. There was no sexual content or conflict to suggest that Ken was battling with his sexual identity. Rather this life seemed smooth and pleasant, without much of the violence and dissatisfaction expressed in many of the other regressions.

Still I have to conclude that Ken was exploring alternative feelings. He agreed. After this regression he freely admitted curiosity about the feelings experienced by the opposite sex. He admitted that maybe he wasn't so baffled by being a woman in his regression.

What did baffle him was the context it was put in. Why was he in a mountain community as part of a nuclear family? That made less sense to him than coming back as a woman.

But that's the way it was.

CHET THE HIGHWAYMAN

Chet's father is a teacher of literature in a southern state college. His grandfather literally owns the town that he lives in. Chet has only been in trouble with the law once, and that was when he was in high school and was arrested—along with several other students—for underage drinking.

He is an athletic and bookish person who reads several books a month.

While many people who are regressed have no idea what country they are in, Chet sensed immediately that he was in England, where he was a bandit. He had the feeling that he was about fifteen years old and already good at his chosen profession.

I was able to see many scenes in which I was holding people up for money.

In one such scene, I stepped out of the bushes in front of a jolly fat man who was riding his horse through the countryside. At first he laughed to see such a young man attempting robbery. Then when he saw me cock the hammer on my pistol he realized that I was serious. With one arm held high, he reached into the pocket of his coat and pulled out his purse. I ordered him to throw it on the ground and then told him to leave.

Another scene had me confronting a carriage with two very regal women inside. I seized their horses and told the driver that I would kill him if the ladies didn't turn over their jewels. They joked and said that maybe he wasn't worth their jewelry. They asked if they could think about it awhile. He pleaded with them until they finally huffed and took their necklaces off and threw them on the ground. Then I let them ride off.

A scene of violence happened when I was about twenty-three years old. I stopped a coach and ordered everyone to get out and stand in the road. One of the men said he wouldn't give me anything, even if I killed him. I pushed him and when that didn't work, I hit him on the head with the butt of my gun.

I must have hit him very hard because he fell down and blood ran thick and heavy from the wound. This sight made me sick and I ran away from the robbery scene and back into the woods where I threw up.

I had the feeling that I lost heart after that and no longer liked my chosen profession.

In the next scene I found myself in London, where I was about to be hanged. The amazing thing about this scene was that the crowd was cheering for me as I was marched to the gallows. I tried to be brave but I was frightened by my impending death. I stood on the gallows and cried as they put the noose over my head. That is all I remembered.

No one in Chet's family has ever been in trouble with the law nor have they displayed the attitudes that arose during his regression. After considerable discussion, we concluded that this was a method for Chet to explore alternative feelings.

He admitted that he had always wondered what living on the other side of the law would be like. This was more than just subconscious curiosity on his part. He had often thought about the workings of the criminal mind.

But, as with Ken, the lifestyle didn't surprise him so much as the context. Why England in what was probably the seventeenth or eighteenth century? To Chet, that was the question that became the real mystery.

THE PERSONALITY-SHOPPING MIND

All of these examples and many others convince me that we have a mechanism in our own minds which seems to help us explore different possibilities.

I know this mechanism exists because from time to time I have sent some of my more neurotic patients "personality shopping." If they don't like the way that they are, I suggest to them that they "shop around" for traits in others that they may want to incorporate into their own personality.

As long as they can honestly do this and not take on neurotic traits, I think it's a fine thing for people to do.

We do it anyway as children. We pick up qualities from our parents, brothers and sisters, and friends. Sometimes these acquired traits bedevil us later in life. For instance, children frequently pick up traits from their parents that they disdain. The old saying, "You become what you hate the most," validly applies to the way children emulate their parents.

From the more mature perspective of adulthood, we can acquire traits more consciously. In doing this by choice, we can be happier and more fulfilled.

For instance, I was once working as a therapist with a woman who didn't have much personality. She came from a big family where individuality wasn't stressed. As a result she had a very bland personality.

Lacking a sense of who she was left her feeling very stressed. When I first took her as a patient, her fingernails were bitten down to the quick. She immediately expressed an anger toward her family and readily admitted that she didn't have any friends and didn't really like anyone in particular. I thought that this attitude said more about her view of herself than it did about the way she felt about the world around her.

I simply told her to go personality shopping. Since she was living in a college dorm at the time, I suggested that she start there. She was surrounded by attractive people so I told her to shop for the personality characteristics she liked.

It proved to be a good therapy for her. Each time she came in for therapy she demonstrated a new trait. The end result for her was a new-found happiness in her life because she was now able to become a person with some identity.

Past-life regressions can represent this form of personality shopping. They allow some people to experience other roles, feelings, and ways of being without outwardly exhibiting a different behavior. Whatever past-life regressions truly are, they help us to harmlessly examine the way we could be.

7

Are They
Hidden Memories?

Two explanations frequently offered for past-life experiences are cryptomnesia and xenoglossia, both of which represent the recall of memory that is hidden deeply in the mind.

Although these do account for the imagery and recall in some regressions, they by no means represent a blanket explanation for the experience of past lives. In fact I find that they actually account for very few explanations.

Nonetheless they are worth looking at as a small part of the past-life phenomenon.

THE RECALL OF CRYPTOMNESIA

Cryptomnesia is the experience of remembering something that is deeply buried in your memory bank. When information like this returns, it usually emerges as a creative product, which means you think of it as something made up and not produced from memory.

An excellent description of cryptomnesia comes from Melvin Harris in his book *Investigating the Unexplained* (Buffalo, N.Y.: Prometheus Books, 1986). He defines past-life regressions as "fascinating examples of cryptomnesia" (a definition I don't agree with) and goes on to explain why:

To understand what cryptomnesia is, we have to understand the subconscious mind as a vast mental storehouse of information. This information comes from books, newspapers and magazines. From lectures, television and radio. From direct observation and even from overheard scraps of conversation.

Under everyday circumstances, much of this knowledge is not subject to normal recall. But there are times when some of these deeply held memories are spontaneously revived. Some of these revived memories revive in a baffling form, since their origins are completely forgotten. This is cryptomnesia proper.

Because the origins are forgotten, the information can seem to have no ancestry and can be mistaken for something newly created.

The late Helen Keller was tragically deceived by such a cryptomnesiac caprice. In 1892 she wrote a charming tale called *The Frost King* that was published and applauded. But within a few months it was revealed that Helen's piece was simply a modified version of Margaret Canby's story *The Frost Fairies*, published 29 years earlier.

Helen Keller had no conscious memory of ever having been told this story. She was blind and deaf, completely dependent upon others for her knowledge. But inquiries revealed that a friend had, in fact, read a batch of Ms. Canby's stories to her by touch in 1888. *The Frost Fairies* was among them.

When this was made public, Helen was devastated. She wrote, "Joy deserted my heart. I had disgraced myself. Yet how could it possibly have happened. I racked my brain until I was weary to recall anything I had read about *The Frost Fairies* until I had written *The Frost King*. But I could remember nothing."

Other authors have been trapped in the same way, as Samuel Rosenberg has testified. Rosenberg worked for Warner Brothers pictures as a literary consultant on plagiarism cases. He records the valuable advice given him by his legal supervisor who said: "Don't be fooled by the sometimes astonishing resemblances you will find when you compare any—any—two films, plays, books, stories or film scripts.

"During the past 25 years we have made hundreds of such comparisons in preparation for court trials. And in a great many cases we have found that both of the quarreling authors—each convinced that he was honest and the other writer an idea thief—had copied their plots, ideas or sequences from an earlier literary classic, the Bible or some forgotten childhood story."

In a similar fashion, a number of automatic writings, supposed to be from dis-incarnate spirits, have been traced to public works. For instance, the great Oscar Wilde scripts of the late 1920s were gradually shown to be derived from many printed sources, including Wilde's own [work].

I agree in part with this assessment. Many of the more elaborate cases, in which a person remembers a past society in great detail, can be linked to this phenomenon. I have experienced a couple of these cases in my own practice.

However, I don't believe this phenomenon is a sufficient explanation for the images in all regressions. As I have already said, there are far more cases that have nothing to do with cryptomnesia than there are that do. Still, I will present a couple of cases of cryptomnesia from my own practice to familiarize you with them.

THE 8-MM INDIAN

Ted was a psychologist in a small southern city who attempted a hypnotic regression out of curiosity. He was surprised to find that the results were a very vivid return to a life as an Indian in an ancient southwestern tribe. Here is his regression. The cryptomnesia part comes later.

I found myself surrounded by buildings made of stone. There were no other people around, but the buildings looked relatively new and lived in.

I was able to walk through this village. There were round buildings that I knew instinctively were religious areas. They were round with a sunken floor and windows placed so that light streamed in majestically. I looked around this room and moved on.

In one scene I was ducking through a doorway and into a room. It was an apartment. There were apartments above us and to the sides. I had the sense that this was my apartment, that I lived there.

In another scene I was standing on a mound of dirt in the middle of this village. I was looking at the mountains around me, the green hills and the valleys that stretched on in the bright southwestern landscape. I felt very free and very much like I belonged there.

Ted was baffled by the regression experience. He had expected nothing like this and didn't really know what to make of it. Why an Indian? Why a snatch of a past life that seemed to have no meaning other than to present imagery? Ted was perplexed.

The source of his "past life" was revealed to him by accident. He was visiting his parents one day and his mother convinced him that they should look at some of the old family movies that she had found in a cabinet.

When the family sat down to watch the scratchy 8-mm films, Ted was surprised to see his regression there on the screen! He had recalled a family trip taken to a southwestern Indian ruin on a car trip across the country.

"It was all there," he said. "The round room that they used for religious ceremonies, the apartment, the distant mountains, everything just as I saw it."

MARK TWAIN REVISITED

Another patient found himself as Mark Twain during his regression. This came as no surprise to people around him who would often remark at how much his humor reminded them of Mark Twain. This surprised the patient, however, because as far as he knew he had never read Twain nor even seen any of the movies made from his work.

People frequently pointed out the many similarities between his life and that of the great American writer. For one thing, he loved sitting on the porch and rocking in a rocking chair. He had loved to do that since early childhood and had never grown tired of it. Twain had the same feelings about rocking chairs.

Another thing he liked to do was sit on the porch and listen to people tell stories. He would encourage anyone he could to tell him a tale. Twain, it was frequently pointed out to him, was the same way.

From his childhood he remembered a traumatic incident similar to one that happened to Twain. His uncle came into the house talking about a man who had died in the local jail. He had gotten drunk—a jailable offense when this man was young—and was put behind bars overnight. While he was in there, the jail caught on fire and the man was burned to death.

My patient recalled that as soon as he heard the story he began to cry. For some reason, he blamed himself for the man's death and was crying from an overwhelming sense of guilt.

Little did he know that Twain took similar responsibility for an incident in which a young man died the same way, in a jailhouse fire.

This patient at one point in his life was also trying to buy a farm in Virginia. Next to the house was a hill that he found so inspiring that he decided to have an architect come and draw up plans for an eight-sided office on top of that hill. It wasn't until later that he discovered Twain had worked from an eight-sided office of similar design at his own place in Connecticut.

Another time, this man was walking across a bridge in the deep South. He turned to look down the river and suddenly had a flash that he *was* Mark Twain, drifting down the river on a paddlewheeler.

This patient—a medical doctor by trade—was also a part-time writer of humorous fiction. Many times after finishing a story he found that story lines he followed in his writing mimicked those of Twain. For instance, one of those pieces dealt with Siamese twins, a subject of great interest to Twain.

This patient remembers being fascinated by astronomy from a very early age, latching onto anyone who could tell him anything about the heavens. Comets were especially fascinating to him. He used to follow his grandmother around asking her about Halley's Comet. Twain, too, was fascinated by astronomy and especially that same comet. He even predicted correctly that his death would occur on the return of this astrological phenomenon to worldly view.

I did a regression on this man, asking him to go back to his most recent previous life. Right there on the couch he "became" Mark Twain. I must say, it was like having Twain—or a facsimile thereof—right there in the room.

Was this an example of reincarnation?

As it turned out, no. This man had been forced to read a considerable amount of Twain's work in high school. The experience of being forced to read Twain must have been somewhat traumatic because he had completely forgotten that he had ever studied the author's work. Yet he had subconsciously picked up several of his traits and interests and even recalled much of his work and life as his own during a regression.

Truth definitely is stranger than fiction!

XENOGLOSSIA

Sometimes people undergoing a past-life regression begin speaking a "different" language. Sometimes that language is understandable, such as cases in which a person begins speaking French or German. Other times it is a language that can't be understood, and possibly isn't a language at all but just "babble" that sounds like it.

How this happens is a mystery. Some researchers say that the person had to have been exposed at some point to the language they were speaking, if not through formal schooling then by hearing it spoken on the radio, perhaps, or even at a table next to theirs in a restaurant.

If the language is incomprehensible, yet has patterns of speech, then the more traditional therapists would say that the subject is "speaking in tongues," which is often defined as unintelligible sounds made under the influence of mystical or religious excitement. Some past-life therapists might believe that the subject is speaking in a "dead" language.

Xenoglossia is not uncommon in past-life regressions. Patients will periodically speak in "tongues" or "dead" languages or even French. When this happens, the cool, collected therapist will usually ask the patient to interpret the language for them. This usually induces them to speak in their current native tongue.

One of the most intriguing examples of xenoglossia that I have ever heard of in past-life therapy happened to a hypnotherapist who wishes to remain anonymous.

While living in the Southwest, he hypnotically regressed a noted Indian artist. When the artist went back into a past life, he began speaking fluent French. The able therapist asked him to translate, and in a heavy French accent, the artist began describing his life in Paris.

In vivid detail he spoke of being a composer of no renown, one who worked all day on his music and spent his depressing evenings in small Parisian cafes.

He was able to tell the hypnotherapist about his life from beginning to end. And at any point in his monologue he was able to switch back into the French language.

The hypnotherapist was unable to find any point in this man's life where he was exposed to the French language. Believers would call this a clear case of reincarnation. Skeptics would at least categorize it as xenoglossia.

As an added dimension to this regression, the hypnotherapist was able to trace the name of the composer. He found reference to this man and his work in a music library. He was everything he had claimed he was in the regression: a minor league composer of poor-quality music. Once again, reincarnation or cryptomnesia?

Noted regression therapist Paul Hansen claims to have encountered xenoglossia many times. If the language being used is one that the multilingual psychotherapist speaks, Hansen will respond to them in the language they are using. They most often respond to him in the language they are using in the regression.

Hansen and most of the other past-life therapists I have spoken to believe that "sometimes" these are examples of reincarnation. They also believe that sometimes they aren't. Most often a patient's exposure to a foreign language can be ferreted out in the therapy that follows a regression. Then the experience can easily be divided into two categories: xenoglossia and "other."

HYPNAGOGIC STATES

Another state of mind that regressions are frequently attributed to is that of hypnagogy, the state that exists between normal waking consciousness and sleep.

This is known as the twilight state, which means one is neither asleep nor fully awake. These hallucinations are different from dreams. Dreamers take part in the events as though being fully engulfed in them. In hypnagogy, the person watches what is being dished up by his unconscious, yet is usually aware of his real surroundings.

A high percentage of the normal population has experiences of vivid imagery at the point of sleep. Sometimes these take the form of colorful images, sometimes surrealistically distorted events. In other cases, the hypnagogic imagery will take the form of little dramas that are played out. People see scenes and faces engaged in various types of activities.

For example, a patient I'll call Patty had a vivid and unexpected regression in which she was a priest in medieval Japan. Her experience occurred through the use of a crystal ball, or by *scrying*. Crystal gazing offers the surest entrance into the state of hypnagogy. Here is her rendering of that experience.

> I saw a complex of houses that were down by a bridge that crossed a river. I knew that I was in Japan by the look of the buildings.
> I was a man in this lifetime. When I came into this one, I was about forty years old. I was working on what

looked like a manuscript, which made me think I was a priest in this town.

At one point I was walking down a road with two younger men who were dressed like monks. There was one on either side of me. We were walking down a beautiful, tree-lined road. The trees were stately and lovely. As I looked into the ball the trees would actually move by me like I was watching 3-D television.

The next scene wasn't so beautiful. I saw the town I was in being consumed by fire. There was fire all around. I could see the flames leaping up and I could see people running and weeping. I felt sorry for them, but from my perspective I knew that they would move on to another existence.

Still I felt sorry. After the fire I had to deal with many people who were depressed and saddened over their losses. In watching this scene, I felt a real need to learn more about how to help people through disasters and stressful events in their lives. As this priest, I didn't really know how to help people wounded by reality.

At that point I was directed to the last scenes in my life. I found myself lying in a house surrounded by people from the community. I was an old man. I rose up and looked down and could see an enormous swelling on the right part of my abdomen. I don't know what it was. I do know that I was weak and delirious.

As I lay there dying, I was able to look back with fondness on my life. It was one of great peace and cheerfulness.

Her experience fits the definition of hypnagogy. To begin with, the images she saw in the crystal ball were unnaturally clear. Later she described several of the scenes as being bright, almost glowing.

Other people report hypnagogic hallucinations as being pictures or patterns that change rapidly. Some people see rapidly shifting scenes almost as though they are looking at pictures from a slide projector. Some see horrible faces and demons, yet few people report being frightened by them.

Where Do They Come From?

When we near a state of sleep, we are on a level of imagery that seems to be going on constantly.

Hypnagogic states are linked with creativity. Some of the world's great creative geniuses have learned to tap into this state to help solve their creative problems. They simply close their eyes and completely relax. The images follow.

The chemist Kekule is one famous example of this. He was researching the structure of the organic compound benzene, a mystery since no one could determine how its six carbon atoms were put together.

One evening while working on this problem he dozed off in an easy chair in his living room and slipped into the hypnagogic state. As he looked before him, he saw images of what looked like snakes whirling around in the air. As he watched, these snakes would go straight and then turn and bite one another on the tails, forming a circle.

From this he figured out that benzene was formed as a ring.

Thomas Edison was another thinker who used this technique in his creative process. It was well known among Edison's associates that when he had a problem that he couldn't solve, he would catnap in his office. There he had a chair in which he could lean back and go into the hypnagogic state to reach solutions.

One problem that he faced is that it is very easy to drift into full sleep from the hypnagogic state. Once asleep, one tends to forget the images experienced. To overcome this problem, the inventive Edison devised a way of awakening himself at the critical time. He held a steel ball in each hand. On either side of his chair, he placed metal dishpans. When he started to drift from the hypnagogic state and into sleep, his hands relaxed and the balls clanged down onto the pans. He would then awaken, often with the solution to the problem.

I am inclined to believe that imagery from past-life regressions sometimes comes from the hypnagogic state. As one drifts into this state, he or she tends to come up with very colorful, very complex images. It is my feeling that regression hypnosis—particularly crystal-ball gazing—frequently guides the subject into this hypnagogic state.

SOME ANSWERS, MORE QUESTIONS

But do these three states—cryptomnesia, xenoglossia, and hypnagogy—explain the source of all past-life regressions? I don't think so. Although they do help to explain some of the qualities inherent in past-life investigations, these states are present in a very small percentage of these experiences.

Nonetheless, they do serve to explain some of the past-life mystery.

8

Do Past Lives Tap Our Personal Myths?

Some intriguing psychological research shows that each of us lives a personal myth. Much like an actor on a stage assumes certain roles, so do we. We are sort of character actors in the play of life.

Many researchers have found these myths to be so similar to those of the ancient Greeks that they can be compared to them by name. So there are people whose lives as they describe them are somewhat akin to Athena's, for instance, the wise goddess of women's crafts who frequently functioned as a peacemaker (that describes many women I know). Or there are many Apollos, people whose descriptions of themselves would place them in the role of prophet and poet. These personal myths help shape a person's life, allowing them to better understand their goals and purposes.

Although these researchers have not dealt with past-life regressions, I find that personal myth seeps out in many of these experiences, especially if one doesn't believe in reincarnation. The stories and images that make up these regressions can be metaphors for the way people see themselves. Analyzed properly, they can help the therapist understand his patient and the patient understand himself.

MYTHS ARE THE SAME

The late mythologist Joseph Campbell found that the same basic characters can be found in the myths of cultures around the world, from the ancient Greeks to the Navajo Indians. These universal characters are even seen in the movies of today. For instance, Campbell noted that King Arthur of the Round Table lives today in the form of Luke Skywalker of *Star Wars*. Hercules has been resurrected as *Rambo* and Aphrodite as the lovely mermaid in *Splash*.

As Campbell expressed in his classic *The Hero with a Thousand Faces*, "The latest incarnation of Oedipus, the continued romance of Beauty and the Beast, stands this afternoon on the corner of 42nd Street and Fifth Avenue, waiting for the traffic light to change." Meaning of course that the characters of myth are all around us, always repeating themselves in slightly different forms.

This means that they are inside of each of us, too.

Dr. Dan McAdams of Loyola University in Chicago probes the unconscious mind by having people tell their own stories in two-hour sessions. He probes them during these sessions, focusing on the main events and most important characters in their lives.

McAdams and his associates then analyze the transcripts of the taped interviews for the consistent themes in each of the stories. By following this process, McAdams is able to come up with the mythic character that is at the center of a person's life. Jungian psychologists call this mythical person the *archetype*. McAdams calls him the *imago*.

Although Dr. McAdams acknowledges that he could use the mythical characters of many cultures (even Hollywood), he chooses those of the ancient Greeks because they are most familiar. Here are the imagos or archetypes that he uses and the definition of each:

Apollo, the healer: Prophet, artist, protector, organizer, legislator.

Athena, the counselor: Arbiter, therapist, teacher, guide, peacemaker.

Prometheus, the humanist: Defender of the weak, revolutionary, evangelist.

Zeus, the ruler: Judge, conqueror, seducer, creator, sage, celebrity.

Hermes, the swift traveler: Explorer, adventurer, trickster, rabble-rouser, persuader, gambler, entrepreneur.

Ares, the warrior: Fighter, soldier, policeman.

Demeter, the caregiver: Altruist, martyr.

Hera, the loyal friend: Spouse, helpmate, chum, confidante, sibling, assistant.

Aphrodite, the lover: Charmer, seducer.

Hestia, the homemaker: Domestic, ritualist.

Hephaestus, the wage-earner: Craftsman, laborer.

Dionysus, the escapist: Pleasure-seeker, hedonist, player, epicure, child.

These archetypes begin in early adulthood, says Dr. McAdams, and change over the years as a person matures. So a person may identify with a warrior or lover archetype early in life and go on to identify with a spouse or helpmate later on. These archetypes change as people find it necessary to reorganize their lives around different principles. A college football player, for instance, may identify with Ares the warrior during his playing years. Later, though, when married and raising a family, he may find himself identifying with Hephaestus the wage-earner. And an Aphrodite (the seducer) can become a Hestia (the domestic) at the drop of a wedding vow.

Although Dr. McAdams doesn't deal with hypnotically regressed subjects, I have found that the past-life experiences of many of my patients resemble the mythological characters of the ancient Greeks. Assuming that these regressions don't represent real past lives, these experiences probably function to engrain one's character into the unconscious mind. They also confirm certain character traits to the unconscious.

I have found that the images and stories one comes up with

over the years can change. Although a patient can always recall any given past life, they can also reveal new ones as they change.

One of my patients as a college student was very much a pleasure-seeking Dionysus in both her current and past lives. Later, when she married and had a regular job, she became much more the spouse and helpmate in both her current life and past-life regressions. She became like Hera.

So in her early past-life experiences, this patient was a footloose dancer in some ninth-century European culture. In her later regressions, she was a happy shop owner who worked alongside her husband in Ireland.

ICARUS (OF SORTS) REVISITED

One of my favorite case studies linking myth to past-life regressions involves a social worker turned truck driver who, during his regression, became a man obsessed with discovering the secret of flight. With a couple of exceptions, his tale is reminiscent of Icarus, who attempted to escape from prison by flying with wings of wax. In that tale, his wings melt when he flies too close to the sun and he falls to his death in the sea.

My patient felt imprisoned in his current life too, although he was imprisoned not by walls but by an unhappy job situation and a bad marriage. He wanted to escape these feelings and regain his lost self-esteem.

All of these feelings take metaphorical and mythological form in his regression.

I found myself in the study of a palatial home. It was in medieval times in perhaps southern France or Italy. I was aware that I had inherited this home from my family and that I was the last family member except for an old doddering uncle who lived in another part of the house. I could see him in this regression. He was old and sick, with heavy jowls and a bald head. His skin was pale and yellowish and he didn't leave his room very much.

I would guess that I lived in a beautiful villa, but I

was only interested in one part—the study. I seemed to spend all of my time in that one room. Looking around I could see a lot of chemistry apparatus, tubing and flasks and burners.

I was obsessed with the idea of flying. My entire interest in life was that one thing. I saw gravity as a prison to be escaped.

On the drawing table before me were large drawings of birds in flight. One of my activities was to watch birds and then draw the shapes of their wings and their bodies in flight.

All around me in this study were leatherbound tomes. I was able to go to the shelf and open one of them up. All of them were handbound works of art. None of them were printed. They were all done by hand.

There were other things in this study, too. There were models of wings and mechanical apparatus designed for flight. There were flying insects and birds all around, too.

In this regression I am reading tales of flight from the Bible, trying to use the scriptures to solve the riddle.

I was a recluse, I spent almost my entire time daydreaming about flight or designing and building flying machines that ultimately didn't work.

In my study is a glass door that looks through a courtyard and out onto a lane that runs by the house. Very often during the day, people walking along the lane shout derisive comments at me. I could hear a child who stopped out there. "Here dwells the man who wants to fly among the birds of heaven." Then he laughed loudly and pointed at me. On the whole, everyone in this town treated me like a heretic, even my servant, who was very surly and contemptuous when he performed work for me.

Frequently I found myself going out to a meadow overlooking the town. From there, I would test my flying machines or just observe birds in flight. I loved watching things that could fly. It seemed a total mystery to me that I could grasp the concepts of flight but never actually get off the ground. It left me with the feeling that I was being tortured by God.

In another scene I was in my study being visited by the local parish priest. He was greatly disturbed by my desire to fly. I showed him the flying machines that I was building and talked to him at length about the way I thought wings worked.

He sat silent most of the time. Finally he said: "Son, man was not meant to fly. God wants us here on earth." He then promised that he would pray for me.

I was able to go ahead to my death. I found myself watching my own funeral. The amazing thing was that I had left my body and was watching it from above! For the first time, I could fly! I was able to fly all around like a bird and watch as they put my body in the ground. There was a victory in death that felt good even at that point.

This regression helped Larry realize that, in the broader sense of the word, he had a deep yearning to fly, from his narrow life as well as from his lack of spiritual growth. To give him a handle by which he could deal with his problems, I call him my Icarus patient. Such a name gives him a better understanding of his problem. It also helps him realize that—myth or not—others have dealt for many years with the same problems he has.

ARES OF THE JUNGLE

Another of my patients is a fighter in the business world. She is a realtor who consistently sells the most property in her company. She is also a community leader. It isn't uncommon to see her name quoted in the newspaper regarding one political issue or another.

To be a mover and shaker in the town she lives in, she must compete in an aggressive and male-dominated world. So it was really no surprise that her regression made her the king of warriors in a distant culture. I call her "Ares of the jungle," after the fighter/soldier of Greek legend. Here is her experience:

I suddenly realized that I was almost naked and comfortable being that way. I was able to look down at my body and see that I was very black. There was nothing covering me except a flap of animal skin over my private parts.

I looked around at my surroundings. I was in a village that consisted of grass huts. There seemed to be a couple hundred people milling around here, cooking food over open fires and scraping animal skins to prepare them for use as clothing or shelter.

As I surveyed this situation, I felt like lord of all that I saw. I could sense that I was a chosen leader in this community.

The next scene confirmed that I was the prince of this kingdom and the next in line to be the king. I was sitting next to a man who I realized was my father. He was very fat and adorned with bright feather necklaces, bracelets, and a feather headdress. He was sitting on a throne made of the finest animal skins and raised above people who were sitting on the ground before us.

I was sitting on this throne next to him. My dress was ornate, although not as much so as his. We were deciding matters of a bureaucratic nature for the tribe. I couldn't tell what the matters were specifically, but I knew that they were important by the serious looks on the faces of the people at our feet. They were waiting for answers from my father and me, since we were their chosen leaders.

I felt a deep, inner power during this regression. I felt very confident being the future leader of this tribe. I enjoyed the feeling of power and the responsibilities. I felt ready to assume my father's role as king when he was ready to pass it on.

However, there was one scene that was very humbling, which made me realize there was a higher authority somewhere. I was in the jungle alone when I suddenly noticed the sun going black. Of course, I was in an eclipse, but in that life I didn't know what an eclipse was! Slowly the sun turned almost completely black and as it did, fear swept my body. I got down on my knees and prayed to the gods that our sun would return.

At that time I thought that the gods were telling me that although I may be among the most powerful people in my world, I was certainly not the most powerful being in the heavens. I prayed for forgiveness and assured them as I bowed in the jungle that I was aware of their power. Of course I assumed they must have heard me because the darkness soon lifted from the face of the earth.

In a later scene I saw myself as king. My father hadn't died but he felt he was too old to continue ruling this kingdom. I saw myself sitting on the king's side of the throne, wearing the ornate trappings that identified me as the ruler. Next to me in the seat that used to be mine was my father. He was now taking the role of counselor.

I felt very regal and comfortable as king. I truly felt as though I had earned it. I sensed that I had many wives by now and could have as many more as I wanted. There were many children in this tribe that belonged to me, too.

In this particular scene, I was sitting in judgment over some tribal matter. I am not certain what the matter was, but I think it involved a dispute over ownership of a cow or some other type of animal. I was totally comfortable being the judge in this situation. That is all I remember. The overwhelming feeling, though, was one of being comfortable with my kingship.

For this woman, being king was in perfect keeping with her self-image, her personal myth. So much so that for her to be something less would have been a surprise to me. In her real life she is a leader and a go-getter who is perfectly comfortable being at the fore. As she so aptly put it: "I was the same in my past life as I am in my present one."

What most baffled her was finding she was a black man in a past life.

Having been raised in the old South, such an image would be taboo. She acknowledged that in her role as part of the power structure, she would never think of being a "black anything," let alone a black African king.

We concluded that along with her accepted mythical role of king, she was probably exploring an alternative lifestyle as well.

DIONYSUS OF DODGE CITY

And then there's rabble-rousing Walter, a patient who, to put it bluntly, lives to party. He is so fond of a good time that he claims to work forty hours a week mainly to support the forty hours he spends barhopping and throwing parties.

He came to be hypnotically regressed to find out what connection if any his past life had to his present. Remarkably, we found it to be very similar to his current one in lifestyle. Here it is:

> When I came into this past life, I was standing behind a bar, pouring drinks, and laughing heartily at a joke that one of my customers was telling.
>
> I couldn't hear the joke, but I was able to look around at my surroundings and see where I was. I was in a bar in the old West! The place was a sight! There were straight-backed wooden chairs and a few tables that were wobbly from being leaned on so much. I was able to look out the door and see the dirt main street. It was dry and dusty out there, which led me to believe that it was summer. I had a sense that Main Street was a muddy mess during the rainy season. But it was dry now, and the horses and the rolling wagon wheels kicked up an enormous amount of dust.
>
> The streets were active, alive with people. This looked to me like a city of commerce. There were men in suits and women in fluffy cotton dresses. And of course there were cowboys riding by on horses and in buckboards. From the looks of the street scene, I think this was the end of the line for many of the cattle drives.
>
> There was an upstairs in this bar that overlooked the main floor. People would buy their drinks downstairs at the bar and carry them up.

I think I owned this place because I really felt in charge. I was very happy, in part because it was crowded and I was making a lot of money, and in part because I loved being in a large group of people.

I went forward in my life. The bar was very crowded this time. Every bit of space inside was taken and people were spilling out into the streets. It appeared to be a special day because everyone was happy. Several people were shooting guns into the air and making whooping sounds.

I think a cattle drive was ending, because this crowd definitely had the feel of people who were relaxing after hard work. I was enjoying the scene. I remember saying to one of my bartenders that moments like these are the ones I like the most.

A later scene was a sad one. There was practically no one in the bar. I was the lone bartender, dispensing drinks to a couple of fellows who were nursing their beers. The place had obviously fallen on hard times and I had the sense that something had changed so drastically in this town that I would soon be forced to close my doors and go out of business. Outside there was none of the hustle and bustle of earlier scenes. A few people were walking by on the sidewalk, but it was nothing compared to what it used to be.

I was quite sad about this, but I knew that closing the bar down was the only thing I could do. I remember standing there at that bar, thinking about all the good times and feeling very happy that I had at least been able to see them.

The results of Walter's regression didn't surprise me. Assuming that his past-life regression wasn't reincarnation, I find it interesting that he sees an end to his party days, an end that has him looking back wistfully on those days of, well, wine and roses.

To Walter, the belief that "all good things must end" is an important part of the party ritual. It is that very belief that is an integral part of partying. "Looking back on the good times from the perspective of the bad is part of what it is all about," he put it succinctly.

Walter's personal myth was well-represented in his regression.

DEMETER THE MARTYR

Sandy lives in a small town where she is known as the town athlete. She works in a store there and spends her free time running, cycling, and involving herself in some team sports.

She lives with her parents with whom she shares fundamentalist Christian beliefs. Outwardly she appears to be happy. Yet her regression tapped some dissatisfaction and a sense of being a martyr that led to some important psychotherapy for her. Here is Sandy's regression:

> I was a young man who seemed to be living in a city. There were very nice white-washed buildings around. I lived in a second-floor apartment above a store that was located on a very narrow street.
>
> There were a few tables and some slightly elevated mats to sleep on. Outside there was running water in a trough that everyone shared, so we seemed to be a very civilized society.
>
> In one scene I was lying in bed listening to all the people outside. There was so much noise and hustle and bustle that I could practically feel the heat of this city.
>
> I found the people outside to be very unruly and pushy. I think this attitude exists because we are in the very poor section of town and the poor people in this society act this way.
>
> In one scene I found myself walking along the street. The streets are dirt that is tightly packed and not very dusty. There are stores all along the way, things like bakeries and wine stores.
>
> In one store I stop to look at the metal scales that grains are weighed on. I am intrigued by their appearance.

They are that greenish-copper look that oxidized copper takes on. The man in this store is weighing out some kind of grain or cereal.

The man that I was in this regression was a very aggressive and hostile fellow. At one point I was sitting in the apartment with my mother, who was very worried about a nagging cough that she was experiencing. She was feeling weaker and weaker and was afraid that this problem was a very bad illness. I was trying to be the tough guy and downplay the illness, but I could see from the look on her face that she was really very sick. Inside I was worried.

The thought of going out to see a doctor wasn't even in our consciousness, which makes me think there was no medical establishment. Instead we asked the neighbors what to do. They were able to advise certain folk remedies, but for the most part they were worthless.

I moved forward to another scene. I was able to see that my mother had died and was stretched out on a table. She looked so lifeless as she lay there. For a few moments I allowed myself the luxury of tears. I felt very confused and distressed by the loss of my mother. Without her, I had no parents left.

Not long after my mother's death, I found myself in a market. I was standing next to an old man who was carrying a large sum of money in a purse. I simply walked up to him and hit him. Then I stole the money! It was as though I wanted to get caught and jailed.

I was arrested and taken to a judge. I was in a line of people who were in chains. The judge would talk to each of us individually and then pass judgment. When it was my turn he pronounced me immediately guilty and sent me out with a work crew.

I was marched far away with a big work crew. We were sent high into the mountains and forced to work in a mine. I don't know what it was we were mining. It was a dirty gray substance but I didn't know what it was and didn't really care. I was just trying to keep working so the guards wouldn't hit me.

We lived in a tight barracks where it was very difficult to sleep. Some men were moaning and screaming all night and others were sitting up gambling all night.

I had a friend who was from another country. He was captured by soldiers and brought here. He was very homesick for his family, especially since we both realized that we were going to die there. This made us very sad and longing for comfort. We found a lonely corner of the barracks and made love.

The next day when we were down in the mine, my friend became extremely upset at a cruel guard. When this guard began yelling at him, he turned and hit him between the eyes with a heavy wooden mallet.

The other guards rushed in and grabbed both of us. They dragged us from the mine and forced us to build crosses of wood. Then they crucified us at the mouth of the mine so all the other workers could see us as they came out from work. The pain in my shoulders from hanging on this cross was amazing and excruciating. The last thing I remember was staring at the opening to the mine and slowly losing consciousness.

As I lost consciousness, I realized that the reason I stole from that old man in the market was that I was having a grief reaction to the death of my mother.

Sandy was very upset by this regression. The crucifixion event struck her as being very sacrilegious. She relaxed greatly when I told her that being hung on a cross was a means of execution applied to many people, not just Christ.

We then worked on the regression, which didn't seem to tie in to her life in any way. She isn't enslaved by her family and on the whole she likes her parents. However, upon further discussion I found her to be passive dependent. These people let everyone else make their decisions because they have a great deal of difficulty with self-assertion. Passive dependence often leaves a person feeling martyred, especially when they ultimately don't like the decision that was made for them.

There were many passive dependent traits exhibited in this regression.

In her mind, crucifixion was a martyr's death. Assuming that this wasn't a reincarnation experience, death on a cross and martyrdom are closely linked.

Her quiet anger marked by explosive outbursts is another trait of the passive dependent.

This regression allowed Sandy to freely discuss her passive dependence. She didn't believe that what she experienced was really reincarnation. She did believe, however, that her regression provided a forum for the expression of her problem.

THERAPEUTIC VALUE OF MYTH

Past-life regressions aimed at discovering personal myth help us get to the very heart of a person's identity. Why is this important?

If you see therapy as a process of understanding a person's story, then regressions that reveal personal myth cut right to the core of identity. These myths give people handles with which they can get a hold on their lives.

For example, a person who finds himself childlike in previous lives, or one who is frequently in hedonistic situations as he goes through his regression, may well be irresponsible and hedonistic in his present life. Such a revelation through regression would illuminate problem areas in a person's life that could then be worked out in therapy. Let me give an example of how I might use personal myth in therapy.

A person came to me who was frustrated by his inability to make decisions. Although he wanted desperately to become more assertive in his life, he was unable to do so. As a result, other people were making decisions for him.

Thinking that there might be something in a past life that had led to this uncertain behavior, he came to me for regression therapy.

I regressed him to a previous life in which this fascinating tale unfolded:

I saw myself as a warrior headed for battle. I was dressed in armor and was carrying a sword. I was in line with at least one hundred other men and we were walking across the desert. We were all quiet and from the feelings I had we knew this was going to be a very bad battle where many of us would be killed.

I didn't want to go to war, but it wasn't only because I was afraid of being killed. I didn't want to go to war because I wasn't sure what side I was really on. We were going to fight people that I liked. I am not sure what the battle was going to be about, but whatever it was, I didn't think the people we were going to fight had really done anything wrong.

I remember thinking that I didn't have to be out here marching to war. I remember thinking that I had a choice. I was mad at myself because I had been swept up in public sentiment. Instead of doing what I wanted to do and not fight for a cause I didn't believe in, I went with public opinion and volunteered for war.

I didn't die in this war, but I did kill many people to stay alive. I was declared a hero when I returned to my home, but I wasn't proud. I was ashamed of all the people I had killed in defense of something I didn't believe in.

This regression reminded me of Hippolytus, who was pitched into a war between the lovely Aphrodite, whom he adored, and Artemis, who was jealous. Because of his passive nature, Hippolytus was unable to say no when asked to go to fight. This connection with myth allowed me to give the patient a story from mythology that would illustrate his problem.

We then set about rescripting this past life. This is something I rarely do, as I pointed out in an earlier chapter. I find that patients are seldom able to accept rescripting. However, I tried it here on a hunch and it worked.

I regressed the patient back to the scene in which he was marching to battle. I had him describe the geography of the land he was marching through and then I had him describe his deepest

feelings of despair about this war and his wish that he not be
involved in the dreadful battle that was about to take place.

When his despair reached its deepest point, we changed the
outcome. I had him step out of the line of soldiers and simply
walk away. No matter what happens, I told him, don't return to
that line of marching soldiers. Here is what happened.

> The commander was summoned and he halted the
> troops and came back to talk to me. At first he ordered
> me to get back in line but I refused. I said I had volun-
> teered to fight and now I was volunteering not to fight.
> He said I couldn't do that but I just ignored him and kept
> walking. He said I was a coward and called me names. I
> kept walking. I was afraid he might kill me as an example
> to the troops but he didn't. He went to the head of the
> line and ordered everyone to start marching again. Most
> of them did. But surprisingly I was not the only person to
> return to my city. Many of the other soldiers felt as I did,
> that this war was a waste of time and life. By refusing to
> fight, I became the impetus for them to take a stand.
>
> Another surprise was that we were not treated like
> cowards when we returned. Others in the city were not in
> favor of this war, either. Our return helped them speak
> their minds about this senseless brutality.

The patient felt good about rescripting this regression. By doing
this he was able to feel what it was like to make his own decision
and able to see the changes that a different decision would produce.

Discovering his personal myth and working with it allowed this
patient to make significant changes in his life. He became more
decisive and satisfied that he was living his life the way he wanted.

Joseph Campbell calls myths the public dream and dreams
the private myth. By successfully tapping these myths through
past-life regressions, it is possible to understand and even alter the
psychological truths that may be hidden or repressed in the
unconscious.

IV

—

Self-Explorations

9

Exploring Your Own Past Lives

There is a belief on the part of some people that exploring past lives is something only certain people can do, that you have to have a special knack. I have found from my own research that this is not true. There are ways that almost anyone can do these regressions. Many patients have told me before trying a regression that they aren't the type to be hypnotized, or that they are too well-grounded to experience anything so "flaky" as a past-life regression.

They then prove to be excellent subjects, capable of deep hypnosis and rich imagery.

But before attempting a past-life regression, I think it's important to go deeply within and find the reasons for wanting to examine your past lives. Why do I want to do this? What do I want to get out of it?

It's best that these be done as an attempt at self-understanding since they can be great tools in trying to figure out why you have phobias or even character problems.

I also suggest that you contact a local past-life therapist or guide. Choose someone who is interested in using these experiences to help you solve or understand present-life dilemmas. Past-life therapists committed to proving that these experiences are proof of reincarnation might miss some helpful links to a person's present-life problems.

HYPNOSIS: YOU'RE ALWAYS IN CONTROL

I can't think of a single other psychological phenomenon that is so confused in the public eye with magical beliefs and myths as hypnosis.

I use hypnosis in my own practice and am constantly amazed at the fear with which it is greeted by patients. By and large, when you bring patients in for hypnotherapy—whether to teach them relaxation or to recover an unconscious trauma—they will often try to refuse the therapy. One of the most common fears is that the hypnotist has them under his power, making them into automatons or slaves.

Actually, nothing could be further from the truth. You can't go into a trance unless you decide you want to, making all hypnosis self-hypnosis. The hypnotist is merely an instructor, a person you go through to enter a hypnotic trance.

Generally speaking, you cannot be forced to do anything under a hypnotic trance that you would not do under waking conditions.

Many people also think that hypnosis is a loss of consciousness and that they won't remember what happened when they are in a trance. Again, this is wrong. Hypnosis is a state of increased concentration and relaxation. It is an extremely restful and peaceful state of consciousness.

Most hypnotized subjects are well aware of what is going on around them in the room, unless they have accepted the suggestion that they will not pay attention to their surroundings. In a way, hypnosis is a state of heightened awareness of inner feelings and processes.

One of the most common reactions I have from people I bring out of hypnosis is, "Well, I don't really know if I was hypnotized or not." They expect it to be something bizarre or magical, when it is merely a state of relaxation that focuses them on internal stimuli.

There is nothing dangerous about hypnosis. In fact, it is one of the safest psychological procedures we have.

Another mistaken impression about hypnosis is that you can't tell a lie while under a trance. Because of the media's interpretation of the trance state, many people think that everything said while in the hypnotic state is truth.

As a matter of fact, it is well established in the psychological literature that lying is perfectly possible while under hypnosis. That is why we have to avoid the belief that because people come up with these elaborate past-life stories while under hypnosis, they must actually be past lives.

TRANCE LOGIC AND OTHER SIGNS

That these experiences can be so vivid is a function of the brain's *trance logic*, its ability to believe two very contradictory things at once. So when you are hypnotized and in a past-life regression, one part of you is perfectly aware that you are living in the present. At the same time, another part of you is convinced that you are in, say, China in the 1600s. It can be a very convincing experience.

Trance logic is one of the signs of deep trance. Here are the signs of hypnosis that may be experienced by the subject. Keep in mind that you may not have all of these feelings. But you can expect one or more if you are truly hypnotized.

✳ A feeling of relaxation that is so deep, you have no desire to expend any effort.

✳ Feelings of heaviness, especially in your arms and legs.

✳ Feelings of numbness, tingling, or dullness in your feet or hands.

✳ A floating sensation.

✳ A sense of being detached from the environment in such a way that surroundings feel quite distant.

I have found that past-life experiences are helped by the ability to enter a fairly deep trance. It is generally a good idea to become comfortable with hypnosis before entering a past-life state. That's why I suggest that you don't attempt to regress the first few times you enter self-hypnosis.

In order to help you do this, there is a sample hypnotic induction technique in the back of the book. Read this through a few times and then read it into a tape recorder, pacing yourself slowly. Hearing your own voice on the tape should ease concerns about loss of control.

When you decide to regress, get into a comfortable room and a comfortable position in which you feel at peace and at ease. Eliminate all distractions. Turn the phone off. Turn the lights down. You might have a single candle to provide soft illumination. And remember, privacy is important.

FORM INSIGHTFUL QUESTIONS

Begin by clearly formulating questions that you need to have insight on before going into the hypnotic trance. For instance, you might ask yourself, "Why am I having such difficulty in my personal relationships?" Or you might wonder, "Why do I have such a phobia about animals?" Keep the questions simple and clear.

Then take off your shoes and get comfortable on a sofa or mattress. Put your hands by your sides and make sure that your legs aren't crossed. You might even want to cover yourself with a blanket, since hypnosis makes your body temperature drop.

At this point, turn on the tape and follow your own instructions.

DIGEST THE EXPERIENCE

When the experience is over, lie there and reflect on what you have learned. You might even want to tape-record your impressions or write them down in a journal. Don't do this so the experience can be filed away and forgotten. Think about it frequently, trying to relate the past-life experience to experiences in your present life.

It might also help at this point to discuss your experiences with sympathetic friends. I even know of groups that meet on a regular basis to discuss their past-life experiences. All of this helps us understand our intricate inner workings.

SCRYING'S GAZING POWER

I have found another method of past-life discovery, one that is much easier and more convenient than self-hypnosis. It is the method known as *scrying*.

Over the years, my involvement in psychology has been extensive. I was a philosophy major in college and even went on to receive a doctorate in that subject. I went to medical school and on into psychiatric training. I have worked in psychiatric hospitals and eventually went into private practice. Through all of this, it wasn't until recently that I even heard of scrying.

I discovered it while perusing the dusty shelves of a used bookstore in Atlanta. I was looking at the titles when one caught my eye. It was entitled *Crystal Gazing,* by Ernest Schal, published in 1905. As I looked through the first few pages of it, I could tell that the writer was a compulsive stickler for details who was not an impressionable or suggestible person. In those pages, he described his studies in this ancient and obscure art.

Scrying is the technical name for crystal-ball gazing. According to the author, cultures as far back as the ancient Egyptians have done it to find answers to questions that are plaguing them.

Scrying has a venerable history. In the Middle Ages in Europe there were scryers who traveled the countryside gazing into mirrors. They would set up tents in towns and gaze into mirrors, providing visions for people who had questions they needed answered. Scrying was also used for divining the future and for criminal detection. When goods were stolen, a person would visit a scryer who would gaze into the mirror and ask who committed the crime. A face would eventually appear to him and that was the person who was accused.

Lost objects were also subject to search by scryers. A person would provide a description of the object and the scryer would use the mirror as a sort of psychic lost and found.

The Catholic Church eventually outlawed scrying for its seemingly mystical properties and it practically disappeared from the Western world.

It has had occasional periods of renaissance, though. A man named Dr. D came across an obsidian mirror that had been used for scrying by Aztec priests. He developed the art of scrying in England, where he attracted the attention of Queen Elizabeth I. She consulted Dr. D regularly to look into his "shewing stone" and get the answers.

Unfortunately, scrying once again got a bad name through its use as a tool for fortune-telling. This tainted image led it to be scratched from the list of acceptable psychological phenomena.

Why would something like this be considered unacceptable? I think Carl Jung summed it up in a passage about our unconscious being.

"It may be difficult for the unprepared reader to understand why facing the unknown in ourselves is a dangerous enterprise. Only experience can teach one what a terrifying enterprise it is to turn away from the familiar affairs of our conscious world and face the entirely unknown in the inner unconscious world."

I think scrying dropped out of Western society because it is one of those techniques that might easily bring up things we don't want to know.

The Eastern world has a different attitude about scrying. Tibetan wise men do their scrying in lakes. In that high and treeless country, the lakes are deep and clear, and when the wise men gaze into them long enough they see the answers to many questions.

In that country, the Chief State Oracle stares into a mirror to answer the questions of the cabinet ministers. They sit around him and listen intently as he looks into a mirror and reveals the course they should follow in determining state policy.

We are more familiar with scrying as the crystal-ball gazing done by gypsy women at county fairs. I have always thought that they were making up what they saw in the balls, but the research of Schal made me doubt my assumptions.

DISCOVERING A TOOL

After my own research I realize that visions in crystal balls aren't made up, but are real. A few weeks after reading Schal's book, I purchased a ball of my own and set it up on the table. I turned the lights out, lit a candle, and began staring into the clear depth before me.

In just a few minutes, I saw clouds. Then visions appeared. I saw a man dressed in a tan raincoat, walking down a lonely street in the city. That faded away and I saw a beautiful red house high in the mountains with a porch protruding over a cliff. The day was sunny and I could see the blue fog-draped mountains off in the distance.

Then I began to see a woman who is a friend of mine. I saw her face very clearly, just as though she were standing before me. This was followed by a childhood memory of my grandmother's house, with its beautiful wooden furniture and finely detailed woven rugs.

These visions went on and on in a disconnected fashion. The images were uncanny. In one sense it was obvious that the images were coming from within myself. I had no sense that they were coming from anywhere else. And yet these images were plainly projected into the crystal ball in color and three dimensions. It was like a holographic television set.

I spent more than an hour looking into the crystal ball and when I finished I was astounded. Why, I wondered, in all my years inquiring into the human mind, had no one ever mentioned this remarkable phenomenon to me? At the same time, I realized I have always been a very imaginative person. My first thought was that this was a rare phenomenon, one that would happen only to someone like myself.

My next step was to take scrying to my wife, a very grounded person. I called her downstairs and asked her to gaze into the crystal ball. She did it for about thirty minutes and then looked back at me with a grin. "Very interesting," she said. She described many images, some vivid re-creations of her childhood and others from mysterious sources.

This wasn't enough for me. I involved a colleague, a wonderful psychotherapist with a more practical bent than myself. I took the ball to his house and instructed him in this ancient art. He was amazed at what he saw.

I then took four crystal balls to a night class that I teach. I set them up in the middle of the room, dimmed the lights, and played soothing music. After forty-five minutes of scrying, I turned on the lights and questioned the forty students. Amazingly more than half of them had had very dramatic encounters.

One of the students thanked me for this "true trip into dreamland."

Another student, a woman from Pakistan, was moved to tears by images of her childhood in the old country.

Two separate groups talked about seeing the same image. Two students sitting by the same ball described a hooded figure in a long dark robe. Two other students reported seeing a dancing ballerina in the ball who kept time with the background music we were playing in the room.

Several other students said that the images they saw were keeping time with the music, too.

The results were intriguing. I repeated the experiment in another class and found similar results. Nearly half of the students had very dramatic images to report.

FROM THE CLASS TO THE CLINIC

My curiosity led me to use the crystal ball in a clinical setting, and it has proven itself to be an excellent projective technique.

Projective techniques are used to find out what is going on in someone's mind. One example of this method is the Rorschach test, in which a patient is shown an ink blot on paper and is asked what he or she sees. What is envisioned gives a clue about what the patient is thinking.

With the crystal ball, I have found a far purer test, one that isn't structured by lines or shapes. The crystal ball is a clear medium, so I know that whatever a person sees in that ball is a product of his own inner working and not a function of the blot's shape.

I have found several typical images in scrying. One type of image is faces or groups of people, some of whom are known to the subject. These figures will actually go through various actions and scenarios. The subject may also see childhood memories, things that happened so long ago that he or she may not have even thought of them since they happened.

As with hypnotic regressions, the images in scrying can't be directed. For instance, if you were to see a group of people sitting at a table, you could not "tell" them what to do next. Chances are they would fade away if you tried to do that.

However, that isn't to say that you can't set up a "context" for these images to occur.

You can sit down with a crystal ball and frame the experience in a thought, an inner resolution in which you say to yourself, "When I sit down to look in the ball, I'm going to see things that have to do with my relationship to my spouse." Or to a phobia or bad habit. If that is done, then the images in the ball will usually conform to that theme.

One evening I decided to relate this discovery to past-life experiences. I sat down in a comfortable room with the crystal ball and suggested that the images in the ball would reveal a past life that was relevant to my present one.

As I gazed into the ball, a series of images came forth. Amazingly, what I was looking at in front of me was the past life I'd had as a female Chinese artist.

After conducting this past-life experiment on myself, I decided to try it with several patients.

MARGARET OF MANCHURIA

My first one was Margaret, a thirty-year-old who was familiar with past-life hypnosis. I did a few minutes of induction to relax her and then I suggested that in a few moments she would open her eyes and gaze into the crystal ball.

"When you do," I said, "you will see a past life that pertains to things you are experiencing now."

Her facial expressions ran through a gamut of emotions. Sometimes she looked sad, sometimes happy, sometimes very intense. When it was over, she told me this marvelous story.

I was a little girl in an ancient Chinese tribe. We lived in a tent and roamed freely across the plains. Some of my early memories were of my father being very cruel to a horse, lashing out with a whip to get the horse to move. I remember crying at his cruelty and him laughing because he couldn't understand why I was upset.

I then moved forward in this lifetime. I was dressed in leather and heavy boots and wool-like garments. It was very cold and snowy. I was in my teenage years and had the sense that I had become hardened to my environment. I also had the feeling that we were a very close tribe that was terribly cruel to outsiders. I was no longer disturbed by cruelty since I had accepted that that was the way to be.

I moved through other scenes in my life. This tribe was moving along in a vast army. At one point I saw us burning down an inn. We just descended on it like a horde and burned it down.

I saw another scene in which we were attacking a walled city with a catapult that was flinging balls of fire into this city.

As I got older I felt myself worn out by this type of life. I was bone-weary and literally exhausted. I had several children who flocked around me and a husband who was very cruel to the outside world, yet comforting to me. At one point I saw us walking down to the river to get water. It was a little parade of family, the kind you see in shopping centers all across the country.

Finally I saw myself in a tent surrounded by a couple of my children. I was an old woman with stringy, gray hair who was about to die. And that was it.

This regression mirrored her present life in many ways. She married into a very clannish family, one that is understanding of its own but not very tolerant of those outside its own bloodline. Her husband personifies the attitude of his family. Although he is gentle and loving to her, he is not especially kind to the people who work for him in his store. Interestingly, when he catches an employee doing something he doesn't like, he "swoops down on them," and "attacks."

Although this woman has two children, she is interested in having many more, since children represent comfort to her.

DAVID OF THE ISLAND

After Margaret, I scryed with several subjects, each with exceptional results. Another of those is a patient I'll call David.

He is a rough-hewn young man from the rural South. He is not very sophisticated and describes his parents as being the same. His mother is a housewife and his father sells insurance.

David has a very washed-out appearance. His hair is sandy gray, his eyes are pale gray, even his clothing seems to consist of the most colorless attire he can find.

I mention his colorless look only because his crystal-ball experience was among the most colorful I have heard. Here is how he described it after the experience.

I saw a group of people on a beach. They had a fire and they were cooking something that looked like fish. I wasn't that interested in the food as I was the people and the place.

We were on an island and not a very big one at that. I could look up and see the hills on the island behind us. I had a knowledge that I could walk around this island in no time at all.

We were dressed in very colorful outfits that we had dyed on this material that seemed almost like paper. As the people around me walked, the skirts they wore swished like a loose-weave paper. They were very bright colors and clashed greatly with the bright greens of the trees and the sharp reds of the flowers.

In the next scene, I was with a bunch of these people and we were running across the shallow parts of the beach gathering fish that were trapped by the tide. We were happy. There was a lot of fruit on this island, too, all of it sweet and filling.

The feeling among the group was very tribal. There wasn't a feeling that anyone was my mom or dad, but that we were all one with each other. The most amazing thing of all to me was that I couldn't tell if I was male or female. I was just very young.

There was one person that I had a close connection with. He was an old man in the tribe, a cheerful person with a real fat stomach and curly black hair. He was the anchor in my life. I remember sitting by the beach talking with him and feeling very comfortable, but I don't remember what we talked about.

I found it interesting that in the regression he lived on an island and he couldn't grow up. It seemed reflective of his current life in which his parents are anxious and resentful about their son being "out of the nest" and exploring things that they don't really understand. As David put it: "They are always trying to pull me back into the morass," which to him meant that they are trying to keep him at home as their child.

The old man in the tribe that David felt close to was not his father, since he clearly doesn't have much respect for him. Nor could it have been either grandfather, since they both died before he was born. After discussing this point, David concluded that the man on the beach was a kind policeman in his family's community who had been a childhood friend to him.

THE MYSTERY OF MICHAEL

One of the most vivid and paradoxical past-life regressions I have ever conducted is a subject I'll call Michael. His regression was a combination of hypnosis and scrying that is baffling for its complexity and origin.

The best description I have for Michael is that he is concrete. He would appear to be totally in place if he came to your door to fix your refrigerator or deliver milk.

He was raised on a 400-acre farm in North Carolina where he cared for farm animals and spent a lot of time hunting and fishing with his brothers.

Michael is not the cerebral type and readily admits that he has little interest in or knowledge of history. Yet his regression

took him to Eastern Europe in the 1600s. In it, he went from a
wealthy childhood to one of poverty to finally becoming a bureaucrat for the monarchy of Hungary. Here is his description of his
own regression.

The first scene in my regression I saw myself riding
down the road in a coach. It was cold and I was bundled
up and sitting next to my mother. I was looking out the
window of the coach, feeling frightened because we were
in a poor area of town and a pack of dogs was running up
next to the coach barking.

The coach stopped and I suddenly found my perspective had changed. I was outside the coach watching as the
door opened and we got out to go into our house. There
was an old woman dressed in ragged clothing who came
out of our house to greet us.

I saw myself come out of the coach. I was wearing a
brown stitched cap over my head to keep warm but still
some of my hair stuck out from under the cap. My hair
was real black and it hung down toward my face, which
was round and very flat.

I could even see my clothing clearly. My clothes were
ruffled and rich-looking and my parents—who got out of
the coach behind me—were well-dressed and obviously
wealthy. My mother was wearing some kind of jeweled
necklace and my father a fine-looking hat.

As they got out of the coach, my parents weren't
paying any attention to me. They were discussing something in a very animated way. My father was an arrogant
man, very haughty and insecure at the same time.

My mother was very flighty, a nervous woman who
seemed on the verge of cracking like an eggshell as she
talked to my father.

In one of the scenes, I found myself back at the house
in Budapest. I was able to watch as I and my parents went
boating on the river. It was one of our favorite activities

I flashed forward to one of the traumatic events of

this lifetime, my father's illness. He was dying of consumption (tuberculosis). I remember seeing my father gasping for breath in his last hours. I saw my mother freaking out as she watched this horrible scene.

I had a feeling of stark terror at this point in watching my mother. I knew that she was going to be unable to protect me at this time.

Then I was able to recall a period of years in which our money was rapidly spent and our household goods were sold off until there was nothing left but me, my mother, and the bare walls. Then she finally had to sell the house and move in with her parents in the village where she had been born.

I remember being impressed with the beautiful, quaint buildings in this village. But I also remember being struck by the feeling of despair among the townspeople. There was an atmosphere of bad feelings there.

I saw a scene in the village in which there was a flood. I saw me and mother being roused from our sleep and told to run. As we ran up a road to high ground we saw a sheet of dark water rushing through the streets.

We lived through that, but all of our belongings were ruined. Everything from my wealthy early life was destroyed by water.

I couldn't relate to anyone in this town, except a very kind schoolmaster who took a liking to me. He made me interested in learning, which was no small task at this point in my life. My father had always been so insistent that I study hard that he was almost abusive. I saw one scene in which I was trying hard to learn something in a book while my father stood over me and shouted at me because I couldn't understand what I was reading. So I was scarred from that experience.

But this teacher taught me to appreciate learning. The more he worked with me, the more I realized that I should pursue some kind of clerical profession, which I did.

I skipped several years ahead and found myself as a young man, headed to Budapest in a carriage.

I went back to the capital and started working for the bureaucracy. Every day I went to the office from my tiny apartment. Ironically, the apartment was so close to the house I had once lived in that it was a source of strain for me to have to go by that house on a daily basis.

I never married, but chose to live a lonely life.

Instead, I lived to work in a meaningless bureaucratic job. Every day I would go through these heavy wooden doors and walk a long, marble hall to my office. There I would sit all day, sorting tax records.

I was able to go forward to the day of my death, which was in my early forties. Like my father, I died of consumption. I remember observing myself from above as the doctor came to visit. I had become weaker and thinner and less hopeful that I would live. I asked the doctor what the problem was and he wouldn't tell me. But it was obvious from the way I looked that I was dying the same way my father had.

This regression was baffling to both Michael and me. He thought of himself as being too concrete a person to even have a past-life regression. When the result of our work was a complex regression we were very surprised.

We examined the elements in Michael's regression. His mother was a very clear-thinking person, not like the confused, scattered woman in the crystal ball. His father too was quite different from the man in the crystal. He was kind and fun to be around, not arrogant like the father in the regression. Never had Michael experienced floods and never had he experienced the fearful fall from wealthy status to that of a poor man.

Michael and I have examined his regression many times and have never been able to link it to any current distress in his life. As it now stands, this is one of the more curious regressions I have ever done.

SCRYING TECHNIQUES

As you can see, regressions accomplished through scrying are as detailed as those done through hypnotism. The difference in most cases is one of control: The subjects in scrying respond better to the notion of regression because they "control" their regressions with the crystal ball. They don't have to worry about losing personal power, a fear that prevents many people from becoming hypnotized.

Here is a checklist of advice to follow if you plan to use scrying to investigate past-life techniques.

* You need a *speculum* or some sort of object to gaze into.

That should be either a crystal ball or a mirror, but I know of people who have successfully done it by gazing into a pan of water. Scrying can be done with a variety of media. The requirement is that the medium provide a clear depth.

By the way, if you decide to use a crystal ball, purchase an inexpensive one. There are some very expensive balls made with ground quartz crystal, but that is an unnecessary expense.

* If you use a ball, get a stand for it to rest on and a piece of black velvet to put beneath it on the table. That prevents reflections from entering the ball.

* Candlelight is the best type of illumination to use. Try it from different angles and distances. I have found that having the candle about two feet away from the ball provides the right type of diffuse light.

* Follow the same induction technique you would for regular hypnosis. If you tape-record your own, use the one that is in the back of this book. However, when you are relaxed and ready for the regression experience, tell yourself to open your eyes and gaze into the crystal ball.

* Be prepared to spend some time gazing into the ball. Don't expect to see something immediately. Scrying requires the right frame of mind, one that doesn't demand too much, too soon.

The right attitude is one of relaxation. Oh yes, and have great expectations. Many people predict failure for themselves when they try this strange practice. Predicting it will certainly make it happen.

BUT FIRST SOME WARNING

Experiencing past lives can be an enlightening spiritual adventure. But like all powerful techniques of self-discovery, it has its pitfalls. This is particularly sobering to me, since it is my impression that a lot of people in our society are anxiously setting out on inner voyages which only a generation ago would have earned them the questioning glances—or even outright derision—of their friends. I know of several instances in which large groups of people have been regressed into past lives by hypnotists, and other cases in which groups of friends or casual acquaintances have experimented with this technique with very little prior preparation. Given the widespread popular fascination with hypnotic regressions, and the obvious willingness on the part of huge numbers of people to give it a try, there is a need to examine some of the abuses which may result from the misuses or misapplications of past-life regressions.

The following description of some of the dangers inherent in past-life experiences is based on my own work both as a subject and as a guide, and on that of colleagues who have made extensive use of past-life regression in their practices or research.

What follows is not intended to deter well-balanced, informed, and sincere individuals from investigating past-life experiences. It is intended only to give warning about some of the difficulties which may present themselves.

There are five major traps which one must avoid when setting out on a past-life journey. These are: charlatans, obsession with past life matters, unrealistic expectations, escapism, and ego inflation.

Charlatans

The fact that there is an enormous public demand for information about past lives, coupled with the fact that hypnosis is a very easy procedure to learn, has created a situation in which uninformed and untrained individuals set themselves up as "expert" practitioners of past-life regression. This problem is made particularly acute by the fact that only a relatively few professional psychologists and psychiatrists are interested in performing past-life regression, bringing about a shortage of trained professionals who are willing to serve as guides for those interested in exploring their past lives.

However, since most people need the assistance of a guide or a hypnotist to get into a past-life experience (at least for the first few times), a person who wants to embark on this unique voyage must exercise great care in choosing who to entrust in this capacity. The importance of choosing the right therapist can be illustrated by a situation I experienced during attendance at a recent conference of those researching unusual spiritual and psychic phenomena.

One day during the lunch hour, it came to my attention that one of the attendees seemed acutely ill He was vomiting and choking. When he finally composed himself and could talk, we learned the reason for his illness. Incredible as it may seem, a few hours earlier he had been hypnotically regressed over the telephone by someone in another state. During the regression, the unfortunate subject went back to a past life in which he had died by being hanged. He was in effect mentally "stuck" at that point when we saw him choking at the pay phone!

This story is an object lesson showing that past-life regression must be followed by a process which psychotherapists call "working through." What that means is that once powerful emotions or memories have been liberated by hypnosis (or any other technique) there must be a time during which the subject can talk about and reconcile those feelings by integrating them into the larger fabric of their life.

On the whole I would urge you to be wary of anyone purporting to *tell* you what your past lives are. It has been my experience that most people who make such grand pronouncements are really interested in keeping their clients in a dependent or inferior position. Find someone who will guide you so you can arrive at your own conclusions. Also, check the credentials of the people guiding you through your regression. Are they professionally trained and licensed hypnotists or psychotherapists?

My experience has been that the best guides are those who help the subject experience a past-life encounter for him- or herself while helping the subject understand their present-life circumstances through the regression experience.

Ideally, the best guide is one who is fascinated not so much by the tales that emerge during regression but by the ways in which those experiences can help the subject learn the truth about him- or herself.

Obsession with Past-Life Matters

Although past-life journeys are relatively new to our society, there have been cultures all over the world and all through time that didn't regard past lives as mysterious events but rather as given facts.

Many of these cultures warn against paying too much attention to these experiences. Although past lives can emerge during a spiritual quest, these events are treated as scenery on the main road to spiritual enlightenment. The frequent response of these cultures to past lives is to take note of them, learn from them, and avoid becoming so engrossed that you lose sight of your goals in life.

I think this is good advice. I have met people who are so engrossed in their past lives that regression becomes almost an end in itself rather than one tool among many in the road to self-understanding.

A common form of "regression obsession" is found among people who go to great lengths to verify details of their past lives. For one thing, there has been little success in actually tracking down and verifying these details. But for another, attempts to verify these accounts detract from using the regression experience to understand present-life dilemmas, which is what they usually relate to anyway.

Unrealistic Expectations

From time to time, people have come to me filled with the exuberant belief that if only they were hypnotized and taken back to a past life, they would experience dramatic relief from annoying conflicts or problems.

Such expectations are unfounded. Although this happens sometimes, past-life regression is not a panacea for all that ails a person. I believe it is most beneficial when undertaken from a realistic perspective. One who goes into it with a curious, accepting, and open attitude is far more likely to have a satisfying experience than one who hopes for a magical solution to life's difficulties.

Escapism

One reason for the surging interest in past lives no doubt lies in the overwhelming complexity of modern life. The alienation so many of us feel toward contemporary institutions and events provides fertile ground for escapist immersion in other lives and simpler times. It is tempting to avoid facing the difficulties and tensions of the present life by slipping into a past existence. I am guilty of this tendency myself. I find hypnosis a very pleasant state, and when I first started exploring my past lives, I found it alluring to watch these spectacular inner dramas unfold as often as I could.

As beguiling as past-life experiences are, however, the overall experience is much better if one avoids escapism and focuses attention on the relevance of the experience to one's present life.

Ego Inflation

Low self-esteem can be a devastating psychological problem. Indeed, many psychologists and psychiatrists say that loss of self-esteem is the very core of one of the most crippling—and common— mental disorders, namely depression.

So distressing is a shaky sense of self-worth that the mind will sometimes go to great lengths to defend itself against these unpleasant feelings, often resorting to all kinds of unusual subterfuges to avoid having to face the pain of low self-regard.

It is not too surprising, then, that some depressed people occasionally become infatuated with past-life regression as an attempt to cure their lack of positive feelings for themselves. After all, it is easy to see how apparent past-life memories can be twisted into a rather beguiling solution for the woes of a person who feels worthless. "So what if I am not much in this life?" The subconscious mind might well think, "In a past life I was a powerful, wise, wealthy person who was well-respected."

This may seem an unlikely possibility, yet I have seen more than one person captivated by such logic. This kind of psychological defense just doesn't work. We all need to be valuable in ourselves, but that value pertains to our needs in the life we are leading. It is in our present life that we must secure a sense of self-esteem in order to be happy. Appeals to a supposedly happy life in a previous existence just won't work in making us happy here. Thus, to seek happiness here by appealing to a blissful past life is just an illusion. Furthermore, going into a past-life regression with this sort of desperate attitude is a way of insuring that one won't get maximum benefit from the experience.

In my experience, the most positive regression voyages seem to take place when the subject has a relaxed, "Let's see what happens" attitude about the adventure and is not using the experience to shore up a sagging self-image.

People who adopt unrealistic, exaggerated behaviors in order to try to feel better about themselves often appear puffed-up or conceited. This is why it is appropriate to refer to this state as "ego inflation." However, it is important to keep in mind that behavior of this kind stems from deep-seated insecurity. People who try to maintain a sense of security by identifying with a supposed former eminence are really only prolonging their agony by avoiding the deficient sense of self-esteem in their present lives.

Paradoxically, past-life regressions used reflectively and thoughtfully as one tool (among others) for self-discovery can eventually result in a deeper self-understanding, which can actually bolster one's self-esteem.

People who seize too quickly on a past-life experience to renew their faltering self-esteem actually deprive themselves of a more vibrant sense of self which a more reflective exploration of past-life phenomena could help bring about.

10

Conclusions

In researching past-life experiences, I have conducted almost two hundred hypnotic regressions with willing subjects. Some of these people had very vivid experiences during which they traveled back through time and saw themselves in many other cultures and situations. Others were only able to witness glimpses of a past life before they found themselves back in their present one. Only a few, about 10 percent, were unable to see a past life at all.

These experiences were all fascinating, and many had origins that were easy to identify. For instance, some reflected a difficult relationship or hidden neurosis in the subject's current life. Others quite obviously revealed a subject's self-image. So a man who feels insecure in his relationship with women may find himself dominated by women in a past life. The connection is often just that simple.

But sometimes the origins of these past lives aren't that simple to figure out. How can I explain those puzzling few cases in which a past-life regression can be traced to an actual past life? I can't and neither can science as a whole. When these "oddities" (as so many of my colleagues call them) arise, they are usually dismissed as an example of cryptomnesia or xenoglossia, a sort of mental regurgitation of old knowledge. In a world of scientific research that relies upon large groups of people having the same response to a specific treatment, the safest way to handle "oddities" is to set them aside in a category and ignore them until they mount up.

"EXTRAORDINARY CLAIMS"

That is why it is difficult to draw scientific conclusions from my research. It is anecdotal in nature, which in this case means it is people telling their stories. There is often no way to confirm their stories, since such cross-checking requires exact dates from the person having the experience and extensive public records from the period. And finally, there is no real way to account for all the psychological factors: How much of this information is "old stuff" trapped by the subconscious? How much of it is deep-seated problems that manifest themselves as past lives? There is really no way to tell.

After all of this work, I would like to be able to point to something that was proof positive of reincarnation. But I can't make such a claim. As the philosophers of the scientific method point out: "Extraordinary claims require extraordinary proof." As far as reincarnation goes, nobody has provided such proof as of yet.

But still, what most people want to know is this: Do these experiences in any way imply that there is reincarnation?

Reincarnation is alluring to the human mind because it offers the prospect of life itself as being a sort of learning process.

Think about it: We all must recall many painful choices and actions that we have taken that in retrospect we deeply regret. It would be nice indeed if we were given many opportunities to search for love, self-fulfillment, and happiness over a longer process of development than we are allowed in only one lifetime. Life is so complex, so confusing at times, and so difficult for us all that at face value it seems unfair that we would get only one chance to master and understand this profound mystery.

But it is precisely because reincarnation is what we would like to believe that we must be extremely wary of any apparent reported observations or data that seem to support this belief. After all, it is very easy for us to delude ourselves into believing something which we would very much like to believe on emotional grounds.

The recent scientific controversy over so-called cold fusion is an example. It was reported by a Utah physicist that he could produce energy through a process that is much cleaner and safer than the nuclear fusion found in reactors.

As of this writing, however, the preponderance of expert opinion seems to be that his observations were mistaken. No doubt an example, in part, of wishful thinking.

The same may be true of reincarnation. It is such an attractive possibility for so many people that belief in it might give rise to psychologically unhealthy expectations.

We must also keep in mind that reincarnation—if it exists—may be very different from how we imagine it to be. It may even be incomprehensibly different.

For instance, suppose we were to ask a class of pre-schoolers, "What will your life be like after you graduate from college?" It would be a very rare child who could even begin to answer this question with any sort of accuracy or clarity. His or her answer would not even come close to the almost incomprehensible realities that he or she will face after graduating from college. The child's statement would be a woefully inadequate version of his or her life at that time.

No doubt these young children would ignore the complexities that would exist later in life. They would likely ignore the sexual factors in relationships, which are among the most powerful in forming a personality. They would be unable to comprehend the work world or even the responsibilities of caring for a family.

Indeed, if their lives twenty years hence were somehow revealed to them it would seem a distant and puzzling fantasy.

If there is a life after death, then how different must the stories that we now hold to be true really be from the reality of an afterlife? Even those humans who have been revived after near death are unanimous in assuring us that earthly language cannot convey the nature of the extraordinary experience they had when they crossed into death.

I believe that past-life experiences are more understandable in the context of mankind's realization of the historical process.

Perhaps these past-life experiences have some connection to mankind's understanding of history. It is entirely possible that these apparent past-life experiences began as a way of coming to grips with the reality that man has lived with for thousands of years, in many kinds of cultures, and in many kinds of modes. Civilization is mind-boggling, especially with our abilities to look with great clarity from the Stone Age to the Computer Age. It is entirely possible that the subconscious in each of us is struggling to discover where we fit in this long chain of humanity.

Recently I was asked this question: If a trial were held to decide the existence of reincarnation, what would the jury conclude? I think it would rule in favor of reincarnation. After all, for most people these past lives are too bewildering to be accounted for in other ways.

On a personal level, my experience with past lives has changed my belief system. No longer do I consider these experiences "oddities." Now I consider them normal events that can happen to almost anyone who can be hypnotized. At their least, they are deep revelations from the subconscious. At their most, they are evidence of life before life.

11

Self-Hypnosis
for Self-Exploration

Fear of losing control prevents many people from going to a hypnotist or from even being hypnotized.

Although a good hypnotherapist wouldn't abuse his power, it is still best for some people to start on their own with hypnotism so they can learn to feel comfortable with it. That's why I have enclosed a script for a self-hypnosis audiotape. This tape will help the user discover his or her past life. With some people self-hypnosis works with the first attempt. With others it takes several tries. The key to successful hypnosis is patience and perseverance.

Read this script slowly and calmly into a tape recorder, keeping in mind that the purpose of this tape is to induce hypnosis, which requires relaxation. You might want to keep a stopwatch handy to keep the intervals between the suggestions consistent.

Read through the script a couple of times to familiarize yourself with it and then turn on the tape recorder and begin reading the self-hypnosis script.

Self-Hypnosis Script

Move the center of your consciousness—the very center of your consciousness—to the muscles of your eyelids.

(5 seconds)

Become aware that all the tension is pouring right out and you are relaxing.

(5 seconds)

Relaxing.

(2 seconds)

Relaxing.

(2 seconds)

You now become aware of your eyes. Just let your eyes relax. Feel them relaxing and releasing.

(5 seconds)

Relax.

(2 seconds)

Relax.

(2 seconds)

Now move the center of your awareness down to the muscles of the upper part of your face.

(2 seconds)

Become aware of them. Now relax

(2 seconds)

Relax

(2 seconds)

Relax

(2 seconds)

Now become aware of your cheeks. Feel all the tension just drain out of your cheeks.

(2 seconds)

Relax.

(2 seconds)

Relax.

(2 seconds)

Relax.

(2 seconds)

Now become aware of the muscles around your mouth. And your lips. Just feel all the tension come out . . . and
Relax.

(2 seconds)

Relax.

(2 seconds)

Relax.

(2 seconds)

Now feel the muscles of your jaw become loose. You just feel those muscles relax. The jaw drops down from its relaxation.

(2 seconds)

Relax.

(2 seconds)

Relax.

(2 seconds)

Relax.

(2 seconds)

You will find that if you need to swallow you can do so naturally and still remain verv, very relaxed.

(2 seconds)

Now feel the muscles of your forehead. Become aware of those muscles. Feel them relax.

(2 seconds)

Relax.

(2 seconds)

Relax.

(2 seconds)

Now in total relaxation, move back across the muscles of your scalp. Now feel the muscles of your scalp relax.

(2 seconds)

Relax.

(2 seconds)

Relax.

(2 seconds)

Relax.

(2 seconds)

Now move the center of your awareness back to the muscles of the back of your head . . . and the back of your neck. . . . And relax.

(2 seconds)

Relax

(2 seconds)

Relax

(2 seconds)

Your whole head is feeling so relaxed. You become aware of how heavy it feels. It feels so relaxed, so heavy that it is just weighing down into the cushion.

(3 seconds)

Now bring the center of your awareness to your nostrils. Become aware of your nostrils. . . . And feel the air going back and forth.

(2 seconds)

Back and forth.

(2 seconds)

Back and forth.

(2 seconds)

Feel how good it feels to have air going through your nostrils into your nose. . . . Right down your throat and into your lungs.

(2 seconds)

Feel the wonderful movement through your lungs as it moves in and out.

(2 seconds)

Feel how the free flow of air makes you feel more and more relaxed. More and more comfortable. Deeper and deeper into relaxation.

(2 seconds)

Now feel as you take a deep breath—as deep as you can—feel the muscles of your chest wall relax.

(2 seconds)

Relax.

(2 seconds)

Relax.

(2 seconds)

Now take another deep breath in and feel more and more relaxed.

(2 seconds)

And more and more relaxed.

(2 seconds)

Feel the relaxation going down to the muscles of the abdomen. Become aware of those muscles.

(2 seconds)

Relax.

(2 seconds)

Relax.

(2 seconds)

Relax.

(2 seconds)

You are very, very relaxed.

(2 seconds)

Now become aware of the muscles from the base of your neck, to the base of your spine.

(2 seconds)

Pay close attention to all the muscles of your spine.

(2 seconds)

Relax

(2 seconds)

Relax.

(2 seconds)

Relax.

(2 seconds)

Now feel the upper part of your body slowly relax. Feel the weight of it as it unwinds.

(2 seconds)

It is feeling heavy.

(2 seconds)

Very, very heavy.

(2 seconds)

Now begin to relax your shoulders. Your right shoulder. Focus all of your attention to that shoulder and let it relax.

(2 seconds)

Relax.

(2 seconds)

Relax.

(2 seconds)

Relax.

(2 seconds)

Now feel the muscles of your right arm relax. Feel those muscles relax.

(2 seconds)

Relax

(2 seconds)

Relax

(2 seconds)

Relax.

(2 seconds)

Now move the center of your awareness down into the muscles of your right forearm. Become aware of those muscles. Let them relax.

(2 seconds)

Relax.

(2 seconds)

Relax.

(2 seconds)

Relax.

(2 seconds)

Now move your awareness to the muscles of your right wrist and hand. All around to the tips of your fingers. Just let them relax.

(2 seconds)

Relax.

(2 seconds)

Relax.

(2 seconds)

Relax.

(2 seconds)

Now move the center of your awareness over to your left shoulder. Focus all of your attention to that shoulder and let it relax.

(2 seconds)

Relax.

(2 seconds)

Relax.

(2 seconds)

Relax.

(2 seconds)

Now feel the muscles of your left arm relax. Feel those muscles relax.

(2 seconds)

Relax.

(2 seconds)

Relax.

(2 seconds)

Relax.

(2 seconds)

Now move the center of your awareness down into the muscles of your left forearm. Become aware of those muscles. Let them relax.

(2 seconds)

Relax.

(2 seconds)

Relax.

(2 seconds)

Relax.

(2 seconds)

Now move your awareness to the muscles of your left wrist and hand. All around to the tips of your fingers. Just let them relax.

(2 seconds)

Relax.

(2 seconds)

Relax.

(2 seconds)

Relax.

(2 seconds)

Now bring the center of your consciousness over to the muscles of your left leg.

Now feel your left upper thigh begin to relax. Feel this relaxation going down to your knee. Become aware of those muscles and relax.

(2 seconds)

Relax.

(2 seconds)

Relax.

(2 seconds)

Relax.

(2 seconds)

Now feel the relaxation going down to your left lower leg. Down through your calf. All the way out through the tips of your toes. Now relax.

(2 seconds)

Relax.

(2 seconds)

Relax.

(2 seconds)

Relax

(2 seconds)

Notice that your whole left side, from the top of your head to the tips of your toes, feels so heavy, so relaxed.

(2 seconds)

You feel very, very relaxed.

(2 seconds)

Your whole body now is feeling so heavy. It just feels as though it is sinking down into the cushions.

(2 seconds)

And if you feel as though your mouth is dry, you can help that by moving the center of your consciousness right down to the pit of your stomach.

(5 seconds)

Now I am going to count down, from ten to zero. And with each count downward, you are going to be more and more deeply relaxed. Until the count of zero, you will be as deeply relaxed and comfortable as you feel comfortable being in this time and place.

(2 seconds)

Now bring the center of your consciousness over to the muscles of your right leg.

Now feel your right upper thigh begin to relax. Feel this relaxation going down to your knee. Become aware of those muscles and relax.

(2 seconds)

Relax.

(2 seconds)

Relax.

(2 seconds)

Relax.

(2 seconds)

Relax

(2 seconds)

Now feel the relaxation going down to your right lower leg. Down through your calf. All the way out through the tips of your toes. Now relax

(2 seconds)

Relax.

(2 seconds)

Relax.

(2 seconds)

Relax.

(2 seconds)

Relax.

(2 seconds)

Notice that your whole right side, from the top of your head to the tips of your toes, feels so heavy, so relaxed.

(2 seconds)

You feel very, very, relaxed.

(2 seconds)

And with each count downward, you will feel more and more deeply relaxed. Very, very comfortable.

(2 seconds)

Ten. You are feeling more deeply relaxed.

(2 seconds)

Nine. You are deeper, deeper, and deeper. You are more comfortable and relaxed.

(2 seconds)

Eight. You are deeper, deeper, deeper down. All the way to . . .

(2 seconds)

Seven. Deeper, deeper, becoming more and more comfortable. All the way to . . .

(2 seconds)

Six. Deeper and deeper and deeper down. Deeper and deeper to . . .

(2 seconds)

Five. You are feeling more and more deeply relaxed all the way to . . .

(2 seconds)

Four. Deeper and deeper. More relaxed. To . . .

(2 seconds)

Three. Going deeper and deeper into relaxation, all the way to . . .

(2 seconds)

Two. Deeper, deeper, to . . .

(2 seconds)

One. Now deeper, deeper, more deeply than ever before. You are very relaxed. Now we'll go to . . .

(2 seconds)

Zero. Here you are as deeply relaxed as you have ever been.

Now I want you to stay very relaxed and very comfortable.

I want you to imagine that you are in a beautiful place. It is a wonderful, wonderful, comfortable place.

And use the power of your mind to imagine this beautiful spot outdoors. Look all around you and see your surroundings vividly. Picture how it looks and feel the comfort that you have in this place.

(2 seconds)

In a moment I am going to ask you to use the power of your mind and imagination. To imagine, to feel that you rise upward out of your body on this beautiful day. To a point of view several hundred feet above yourself.

From that point, you will descend gradually until you come back down to earth again. But this time, when your feet hit the ground, you will find yourself in a previous life. In an experience that feels very much like a life you have led sometime in the past. Before you were born.

You will be able to see the scenes of your life.

You will be able to go in and out of them.

Even though you are very deeply relaxed, you will be

able to talk and simultaneously the feelings, thoughts, and scenes will come to mind.

And if you wish you will be able to disengage your critical faculties and just let whatever comes up to your mind surface. You will be able to go with it.

Later on, you will be able to look back on it critically and analytically if you wish. But for now just let it happen.

The experience will come. And you will find that throughout this experience your body will be relaxed and comfortable.

You may experience the emotions that come along with any events. And if you do, you'll feel completely confident that these emotions can in no way harm you now.

You have lived through them before and you know you are safe.

Now, from this beautiful spot, feel the life-force in you, that tingling energy in your body.

Now, feel yourself rising up above your body. Use the power of your mind to rise above the level of your body. Just a few inches at first. Now you can feel yourself drifting higher and higher.

Feel yourself drift higher above your body. Use the power of the mind to picture it. There you are. You are feeling so comfortable. So relaxed.

In a moment I'll snap my fingers and your unconscious mind will select a past life which is particularly relevant and interesting to your life now.

Just relax and let your subconscious mind do the work. Let it select the life.

(Snap fingers once.)

Now feel yourself drift slowly down. Down. Down. Now slowly, gently, ready to touch the ground.

Now remember that when you touch the ground you'll remember a past and you'll accept what you see

You are drifting down, down. You are slowly settling down to the ground. You are looking down at your feet.

Can you see your feet?

(2 seconds)

Look at the ground around your feet.

(2 seconds)

Now slowly look up . . .

(1 second)

. . . Slowly . . .

(1 second)

. . . Slowly . . .

(2 seconds)

Be willing to accept what you see.

(2 seconds)

Slowly look up. Be willing to accept what you see.

(2 seconds)

You should be looking straight ahead now.

(2 seconds)

The world around you should be coming slowly into focus.

(1 second)

Slowly into focus.

(1 second)

Slowly into focus.

(1 second)

Things should be clearer now.

(1 second)

Clearer.

(1 second)

Clearer.

(1 second)

Focus now and accept what you see.

(2 seconds)

Accept your surroundings.

(2 seconds)

Now, when I count to three, tell me what you see.

(1 second)

One . . .

(1 second)

Two . . .

(1 second)

Three . . .

(2 seconds)

Now tell me what you see in this past life

(30-second gap on tape)

Tell me more.

(30 seconds)

If you can tell me more, please do. But don't feel pressured. Tell me what you see if you see anything.

(30 seconds)

Are there any people?

(5 seconds)

If you see any, what are they wearing and what do tney look like?

(30 seconds)

What does the surrounding area look like? Talk about what you see. Are there buildings or structures of any kind? What is the geography like? Tell me

(30 seconds)

Tell me more about the surroundings in this past life if you can.

(15 seconds)

Feel free to move around in this past life

(5 seconds)

Explore at will. Examine things around you. Look at this past life with wonder. Tell me what you see.

(30 seconds)

Can you hear any conversations?

(2 seconds)

If you can, tell me what you are hearing. If you can't, don't worry. Just continue to move around in this dream.

(2 seconds)

Describe what you see and hear. I am listening.

(30 seconds)

If you want to continue, I am still listening.

(30 seconds)

Do you hear any more conversations or any conversations at all? Tell me more of what you hear and see.

(30 seconds)

Do you see anyone in this past life who is with you in your present life?

(3 seconds)

If you do, tell me about them. Who are they in this past life?

(30 seconds)

Tell me how they are treating you.

(30 seconds)

You can move through time in this past life. Move to the end of this life and tell me what you see.

(2 seconds)

How do you look?

(15 seconds)

Where are you? Describe the surroundings.

(15 seconds)

I want you to tell me what is happening at this point in your past life. I will be silent for a couple of minutes while you describe in all the detail you can what is happening. Go ahead and talk.

(2 minutes)

Do you have more to say? I will be silent for another minute while you tell me more if you wish.

(1 minute)

Okay. Is there more? I'll be silent while you speak.

(30 seconds)

Okay. Freeze your past life right where it is. You are in control of these events so you can certainly do that if you wish.

(5 seconds)

I want you to remember that this was a past life. You are in another life now and whatever happened in that past life was something you lived through. You can learn to live better and more happily in your current life through the experiences in your past life.

(5 seconds)

You are going to come gently back to your current life. Feel yourself drift slowly down into your body. Slowly. Slowly.

(5 seconds)

Feel your subconscious letting go of the past life and returning to your body. Slowly. Slowly. It is slipping back inside of you like a hand in a glove.

(5 seconds)

Can you feel it? You are back inside of your body.

(5 seconds)

Gently move your hands and your feet.

(5 seconds)

Gently move your head from side to side.

(5 seconds)

Take three deep breaths.

(2 seconds)

One . . .

(2 seconds)

Two . . .

(2 seconds)

And three.

(2 seconds)

You are back now. Open your eyes and become aware of your surroundings. I am finished now, but you should lie there a few minutes more and think about the past life you just experienced. Does it relate to your present life? Are there lessons that can be learned from it? Think awhile and then go on about your day.

(This concludes the tape.)

THE VALUE OF SELF-HYPNOSIS

As you can see, there are certain limitations with an audiotape that don't occur with a live hypnotism. For instance, an audiotape assumes that certain experiences are going to happen, like the subject will see other people in his or her regression or will see buildings or specific geography.

Oftentimes people being regressed don't see these things at all, at which point the blind guidance of the audiotape would confuse them. A live hypnotist would go with the flow, following the lead of the subject.

Audiotape scripts are also unable to anticipate events that might be interesting and pertinent to a subject's present life. For instance, if a smattering of conversation was recalled in a past life that had relevance to a subject's present-life dilemma, the audiotape script would not be able to probe it further, while the live hypnotist would.

So now that I have exposed some of the negatives of audiotape regression, let me tell you its main value: *It makes a subject feel at ease with hypnosis because the hypnotic induction is coming from his or her own mouth.* That is where the true value of the audio script lies. If the subject has a moderate amount of success at self-hypnosis with this self-produced audiotape, he or she may understand that the true nature of hypnosis isn't that of giving up control, but of actually gaining enough control to tap the subconscious.

Such understanding may actually inspire them to further exploration through the talents of a skilled hypnotherapist.